Anne Carter
May 2013

MOMENTS WITH GOD ON

Route 66

DR. DAVID JEREMIAH

Table of Contents

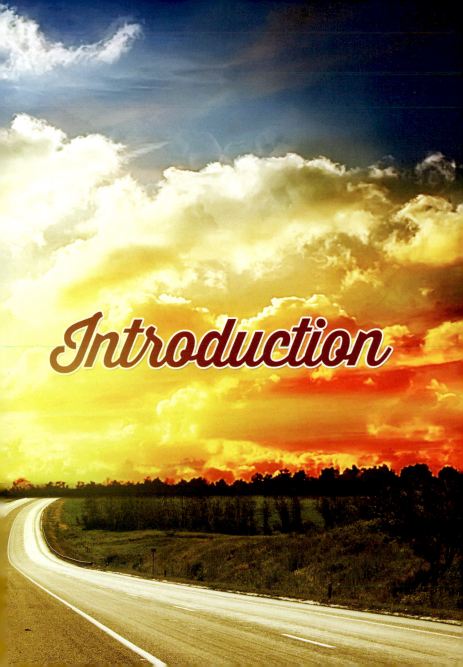

Introduction

Introduction

If you ever plan to motor west,
Travel my way, take the highway that is best.
Get your kicks on route sixty-six.

It winds from Chicago to L.A.,
More than two thousand miles all the way.
Get your kicks on route sixty-six.

Won't you get hip to this timely tip:
When you make that California trip
Get your kicks on route sixty-six.
(Lyrics by Bobby Troup)

When our family moved from Indiana to California in 1981, we didn't take Route 66—though we could have. It was commissioned as U.S. Highway ("Route") 66 in 1926, the year highways began to be numbered. Sadly, Route 66 was officially deactivated on road maps in 1985 and the "U.S. 66" highway signs were taken down.

But in its glory days, Route 66 came to be known as the "Mother Road" of American highways. It stretched from Chicago to Los Angeles (Santa Monica), California. It was 2,448 miles long, crossing eight states (Illinois,

Missouri, Kansas, Oklahoma, Texas, New Mexico, Arizona, and California) and three time zones. It was formed by piecing together sections of local roads and highways, and wasn't fully paved until 1937. Today, Interstates 55, 44, 40, 15, and 10 follow part of the path of Route 66, but most of it remains hidden among the relics of Americana scattered between Chicago and L.A.

Route 66 had it all: old iron bridges, teepee motels, the Cadillac graveyard in Arizona, and more Burma-Shave signs than you could count. Like life itself, you never knew what would appear around the next bend in the road. In fact, anything you needed or wanted to see could be found on Route 66. That's why it was called "The Main Street of America"—there was something for everyone. And those who never got to drive it in person could do so vicariously through the hit TV show *Route 66,* which aired from 1960-1964.

There is another "Route 66," however, that began more than 3,000 years ago and was completed no less than 1,900 years ago. For nearly two millennia, it has been an artery through which has flowed the spiritual life of a kingdom that now reaches to every corner of the world. And unlike the asphalt Route 66, God's "Route 66"—the Holy Scriptures—never needs repairing, never needs updating, never loses its relevance to travelers, and has never been replaced by more modern methods of spiritual transformation.

The sixty-six books of the Bible—thirty-nine in the Old Testament and twenty-seven in the New Testament—are what make up God's "Highway to Heaven." Think of them as service stations or way stations along the road: sixty-six different opportunities for you to refuel, get directions, be encouraged, see historical sights, and be refreshed on the way from your house on earth to God's house in heaven (John 14:1-2).

God, in His wisdom, has given us a road map to heaven with sixty-six parts, and it is important to thoroughly travel all sixty-six highways.

More than seven years ago, I had a burden to reach a non-Christian audience with the Word of God. We created *Route 66*, one-minute radio programs that could be aired on secular and Christian stations alike. God has richly blessed this effort with many coming to know the Lord and the ministry of Turning Point through these short programs.

The following pages reflect much of the content God has used on *Route 66*. It is our desire with this book to reinvigorate you to travel daily on Route 66 and be a student of God's Word. Short and to the point, each of these *Route 66* inspirations packs a strong spiritual takeaway.

So get on the road to new life!

If you travel via God's Route 66 faithfully every day, you'll never lose your way. You'll arrive at heaven's gate on time and by design.

Blessings,

David Jeremiah

Know
THE
Way

Guidance

A man saw a friend of his and asked how he was doing.

"Not so good," the friend replied, "I'm a little confused."

"Why are you confused?" the man asked.

"Well, at breakfast yesterday my horoscope told me to do something, but then at supper last night my fortune cookie contradicted my horoscope!"

Actually, I think that man's confusion began long before he got that conflicting advice. All too often people look for advice in all the wrong places and end up like that man—muddled and misguided. The Bible's advice for all who need guidance is not confusing at all: Trust in the Lord with all your heart, and do not depend on your own understanding. In all your ways acknowledge Him and He will direct your paths.

Trust in the Lord on the road to new life.

Discover God's guidance . . . on Route 66.

Questions

To get her students not to be afraid to ask questions in class, a teacher told them this: A person who asks a question may feel foolish for a moment, but a person who never asks a question will look foolish forever. And that is true in the spiritual life as well.

God told His people through the prophet Jeremiah, "Call to Me, and I will answer you" (Jeremiah 33:3). God is not afraid of our questions. He wants us to seek Him out to gain the answers and guidance we need. If you can't find the answer to your question in Scripture, ask Him directly in prayer.

Ask questions on the road to new life.

Discover God's answers . . . on Route 66.

Instruction

The American male has traditionally enjoyed three distinct venues in which to get free advice: from his barber, his brother, and his bowling buddies. In each setting, just mention a topic and the conversation will begin and continue indefinitely. Solving the problems of the world is what these friends are for.

But may I recommend a fourth source of advice, insight, and counsel that is time-tested, always available, and also begins with the letter "B"? That's right—it's your Bible. There's a reason the Bible is the most printed book in history. Every one of its words is profitable for doctrine, reproof, correction, and instruction in righteousness.

You have a manual for the road to new life.

Discover God's Book . . . on Route 66.

Decisions

If you have ever served on a committee, you will appreciate this observation by American novelist Fletcher Knebel: "A decision is what a man makes when he can't get anyone to serve on a committee." Committees can be very valuable, of course, as long as they are necessary and consist of the right people.

For the Christian, there is no such thing as solitary decision-making, as living life alone. Every decision is always made by a committee of four: the Christian plus the Father, Son, and Holy Spirit. If you are facing a difficult decision today, call your committee together and ask their advice—they are always available.

Decide on the road to new life.

Discover God's counsel . . . on Route 66.

Advice

Have you ever noticed how intelligent the person is who asks you for advice about a particular matter? They're wise alright, but it's not just because they picked you to give them counsel. It's because they were wise enough to seek out advice from others in the first place.

Too many people are afraid to ask for help or advice, but the Book of Proverbs speaks highly of it. It's one of the advantages of having family, friends, and wise members of our church. Nobody has all the answers, and those who have the most are the ones who are willing to say, "Do you have a minute?"

Request assistance on the road to new life.

Discover God's advice . . . on Route 66.

Opinions

Someone has said that the person who doesn't care what others think is usually found at one of two places: the top of the ladder or the bottom. There's a sermon's worth of material in that observation.

Sometimes in life it's necessary to move ahead of the crowd, to ignore what conventional wisdom says. Pioneers, apostles, missionaries, and visionaries fit that category. They have succeeded because they didn't care what others thought—but they are the exception. The Book of Proverbs warns against rejecting wise counsel and predicts calamities for those who do. When you are considering what others think, make sure you listen the hardest to God.

Be open to God's leading on the road to new life.

Discover God's way . . . on Route 66.

Wisdom

If you and I were next-door neighbors chatting in the driveway, one of us would likely mention some unexpected development in our life. Perhaps an extended family member diagnosed with a serious disease, perhaps a child with a special need, perhaps an automobile accident or an appliance gone bad, or the crabgrass taking over the yard!

We face issues weekly, if not daily, that are new for us—situations that prompt us to ask, "What should I do now?" The Bible has an answer: Ask God for wisdom. James 1:5 says if we lack wisdom, we should ask God for it—then believe that He will provide.

Pray for wisdom on the road to new life.

Discover God's provision . . . on Route 66.

Counsel

We hear the words "fool" and "foolish" often enough that it is easy to lose sight of their true meaning. A verse in the Book of Proverbs makes it clear: "The way of a fool *is* right in his own eyes." In other words, a fool is a person who refuses to heed the moral advice of those who are wiser. A fool does what he wants in spite of the pain it causes him and others.

From the Bible's perspective, the fool is a person who refuses to listen to God's counsel or warnings. But the wise person is the one who submits his reasoning to God.

Accept direction on the road to new life.

Discover God's thoughts . . . on Route 66.

Solutions

When Albert Einstein talked about problem solving, people usually paid attention. Here's what he said: "The significant problems we face cannot be solved at the same level of thinking we were at when we created them." That makes good sense. We often need to think differently— outside the box, as they say.

But here's another dimension to consider. The apostle Paul wrote that God is able to provide solutions and answers in life that are beyond what we might think of on our own. If you have a problem today, ask God to give you answers beyond what you might think of on your own.

Be a problem solver on the road to new life.

Discover God's solutions . . . on Route 66.

Hope

Several times the Old Testament psalmist asked himself, "Why are you cast down, O my soul?" It's a kind of spiritual self-talk. He was discouraged, so he interviewed himself to find out why. And he also provided himself the solution: "Hope in God; for I shall yet praise Him" for His help (Psalm 43:5).

Humanly speaking, there are many reasons in this world one might be discouraged. If you become discouraged, be your own counselor. Look for the reason and ask the Holy Spirit to help you settle on biblical promises—biblical reasons for hoping in God. And purpose to praise Him yet again for His help.

Hold fast to hope on the road to new life.

Discover God's help . . . on Route 66.

Stepping Out

The Greek philosopher Heraclitus lived about five hundred years before Christ. He made this observation about opportunities in life. "You cannot step twice into the same river," he said, "for other waters are continually flowing on." Like a river, life is constantly moving forward. The opportunity that presents itself today may be gone tomorrow.

That doesn't mean every opportunity is wise. But it does mean that when opportunities appear, our first prayer should be: "Lord, is this from You? Give me faith to step out or faith to stay put." Proverbs says that if we will acknowledge God in all our ways, He will direct our path.

Step out on the road to new life.

Discover God's opportunities . . . on Route 66.

God's Guide

In the pagan city of Corinth, new Christians struggled to learn how to follow Christ. For example, was it acceptable to buy meat that had been offered as a sacrifice to idols? Was that a sin?

The apostle Paul's answer was that the origin of the food didn't matter. But he gave them a guideline to use in that situation and in every area of life: "Therefore," Paul wrote, "whether you eat or drink, or whatever you do, do all to the glory of God" (1 Corinthians 10:31). That is a guide for life for the Christian. Each day let us ask ourselves: Is God being glorified in what I choose to do?

Follow God on the road to new life.

Discover His guide for living . . . on Route 66.

Dark Tunnels

Life can seem like a dark tunnel. We see a small light ahead but don't know if it's the end of the tunnel or an oncoming freight train! None of us knows what is coming next in life. Therefore, we have to choose whether to walk in fear or by faith.

Life should be a discovery! Even though we can't see the future, God can. The psalmist wrote that God's Word is like a lamp unto our feet. Sometimes we have just enough light to take the next step while trusting Him for the future. If you're walking into something unknown today, trust God to guide you.

Walk in the light on the road to new life.

Discover God's faithfulness . . . on Route 66.

Business of Life

I once heard of a pastor who regularly asked his staff: "What business are we in?" and "How's business going?"[1] The church is obviously not a business, but we have many of the same responsibilities: We have to define our mission, be accountable, measure results, and take care of our "customers."

I think those are good questions for individuals, too. What business are you in? What is your mission in life? How is that mission going? God wants us to know where we are going and how to get there. And He is more than willing to help!

Endeavor to succeed on the road to new life.

Discover God's work . . . on Route 66.

---

1   The pastor was John Wimber, late founder of the Vineyard Association of Churches.

Directions

In the Alice in Wonderland fairy tale, Alice asked the Cheshire-Cat which way she should go. The Cat said, "That depends a good deal on where you want to get to." And Alice replied, "I don't much care where." "Then," said the astute Cat, "it doesn't matter which way you go."

Do we sometimes live like Alice—not knowing *how* to go because we don't know *where* to go? When we fail to discover our purpose, it's easy to get lost or choose the wrong path in life. If you're not sure about the direction of your life, ask God for wisdom. He has the answer.

Know your purpose on the road to new life.

Discover God's direction . . . on Route 66.

Foresight

Hindsight is always 20/20. A better way to say it is that hindsight is an exact science—looking back on a set of circumstances, we know exactly what we would have done or said differently. While hindsight is an exact science, foresight is definitely inexact—at least from the human perspective. For most humans, that is.

There were some men in the Bible whom God gifted with the ability to foretell the future. None of their predictions have ever been proven wrong, which gives us comfort about those that are yet to be fulfilled. While we might not know the future, God certainly does.

There is foresight for the road to new life.

Discover God's perspective . . . on Route 66.

Bearings

No one has embraced the new GPS navigation technology more enthusiastically than boaters. As soon as you lose sight of land, whether in a commercial or pleasure boat, the subtle influences of wind and current can be disorienting. And nothing is more dangerous than being lost at sea.

Nothing, that is, except being lost in life—where there are influences more dangerous than winds and currents. Fortunately, there are good influences for those who know Christ: The Bible, the Holy Spirit, and spiritually mature friends can keep us headed in the right direction. Positive influences: Don't leave home without them!

Get your bearings on the road to new life.

Discover God's plan for support . . . on Route 66.

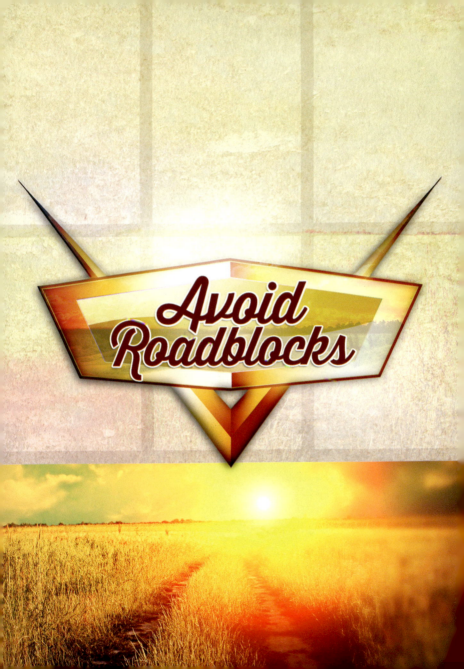

Road to Ruin

When I read a Japanese proverb that said the reputation of a thousand years may be determined by the conduct of one hour, I thought of someone who lived two thousand years ago. For the love of thirty pieces of silver, Judas Iscariot's life was ruined forever—in one night.

I also immediately paraphrased in my mind the words of the English Reformer, John Bradford, who said, "There, but for the grace of God, go I." I am sorry for Judas and his ruined reputation, but I would be even more sorry for mine—or for yours. We must pray daily for the grace not to take the road to ruin.

Choose the road to new life.

Discover God's grace . . . on Route 66.

Unrighteous Living

Because of the number of high-profile leaders and politicians who have had unsavory aspects of their lives revealed, it has become popular to suggest that what one does in his or her private life is not important.

But there is a thin line—perhaps no line at all— between our private and public motivations. If one lives a shameful life in private, it is only a matter of time before it impacts the lives of others in a public way. The psalmist asked God to search his most private thoughts in order that he might walk righteously in public. And we should do the same.

Ask God to search your thoughts on the road to new life.

Discover His righteousness . . . on Route 66.

Foolish Ventures

In 1882 a man named Joseph Richardson owned a five-foot-wide strip of a city block in New York City. He wanted to sell it, but no one offered what he thought it was worth. So to spite them, he constructed an apartment building five feet wide, one hundred four feet long, and four stories tall. Known as the Spite House, it was demolished in 1915.

The Bible's advice is to let wisdom rule in our lives so we don't invest ourselves in foolish ventures we may ultimately regret, like constructing a Spite House that one day has to be torn down.

Be sensible on the road to new life.

Discover God's wisdom . . . on Route 66.

Problems

A college student was complaining to her mother about how hard an upcoming exam was going to be. So she decided to study especially hard for the test. For three straight days she studied, mastering the material. Later she told her mother: "I don't know why I bothered studying so much. That was the easiest test I've ever taken!"

It has been my observation that people who are prepared for life's problems really don't think life is very problematic. Yes, they have problems like everyone—but they are prepared. And they get prepared by studying the Bible—where life's problems and solutions are thoroughly explained.

Explore the road to new life.

Discover God's blueprint . . . on Route 66.

Future Foul

Thomas Fuller was a seventeenth-century English churchman who is given credit for a small piece of common sense. He said, "In fair weather prepare for foul." I call this "common sense" because it seems so obvious. Yet many people do not use the fair days of life to prepare for the foul.

The world's greatest collection of practical sense—the Bible's Book of Proverbs—devotes several verses to the ant that gathers food in the summer to make it through the winter. The ant uses fair days to prepare for the inevitable foul days. And if we are wise like the ant, we will do the same.

Be prepared on the road to new life.

Discover God's common sense . . . on Route 66.

Spiritual Ambush

The Spanish have a proverb that says, "The devil's boots don't creak," meaning the devil can walk right up behind you without your even knowing it. That sounds just like the description the apostle Peter gave of the devil, picturing him as a lion. Lions make no noise at all as they sneak up on their prey on the African plains.

So how do you keep from being ambushed if you can't hear the devil coming? By being sober and alert, as Peter says. By being like an antelope that is continually watching for signs of danger. Alert equals alive when it comes to spiritual warfare.

Stay vigilant on the road to new life.

Discover God's spiritual defenses . . . on Route 66.

Vulnerability

In the ancient world, a city without a wall was issuing an open invitation to its enemies to walk right in. When the Jewish captives returned to Jerusalem from Babylon, the first thing they did was rebuild the city walls. Working night and day, Nehemiah led the workers to complete the wall in an astonishing fifty-two days.

Proverbs 25:28 says there is a spiritual equivalent to a city wall that can protect a person throughout life—and that wall is self-control. A person without self-control is like a city without a wall, making himself vulnerable to all sorts of dangerous attacks.

Guard yourself on the road to new life.

Discover how the fruit of the Spirit produces self-control . . . on Route 66.

Confusion

Modern life can be confusing. There are many things that used to be called "evil" that are now called "good." And many things that used to be called "good" are now called "evil"—or at the very least, they are called "narrow-minded," "intolerant," "prejudiced," or "old fashioned."

But such confusion is not new. God once warned the Israelites, through the prophet Isaiah, about the same thing. "Woe to those," God said, "who call evil good, and good evil; who put darkness for light, and light for darkness; who put bitter for sweet, and sweet for bitter" (Isaiah 5:20). Ancient words that we should heed today.

Pray for discernment on the road to new life.

Discover God's enlightenment . . . on Route 66.

Persuasion

It was the chaplain to the United States Senate, Peter Marshall, who opened the 1947 session by praying, "Give to us clear vision that we may know where to stand and what to stand for—because unless we stand for something, we shall fall for anything."

It has been said that deciding what to stand for in life is the ultimate human decision. And that it doesn't become worth living for unless it is worth dying for. Have you decided where you stand, and with whom? The Bible is full of good thoughts on standards— what's important now . . . and for eternity.

Stand firm in your convictions on the road to new life.

Discover God's perspective . . . on Route 66.

Pride

If you are asked a difficult question, are you willing to say, "I'm sorry—I don't know the answer"? Sometimes our pride keeps us from admitting our lack of knowledge or expertise, and we get in deep trouble by trying to pretend we're someone we're not. I once read that the human mind is like a television set—when it goes blank, it's a good idea to turn off the sound.

The Bible says a lot about pride—how it causes us to stumble and fall. And how God opposes the proud but gives grace to the humble. Humility is being willing to say, "I don't know."

Lay aside your pride on the road to new life.

Discover godly humility . . . on Route 66.

Envy

No teacher or parent knows how it happens, but one of the first things a child learns in school is that some other child is getting a bigger allowance. It doesn't take long for children to get infected with the diseases of comparison, envy, and jealousy—and the condition seems to get worse with age.

Like you, I've suffered through occasional bouts of those spiritual illnesses, but have finally found the cure: a profound sense of gratitude for God's good gifts and the reminder that this world is not my true home. There's nothing like gratitude and thanks to God to cool the burning fever of envy.

Leave bitterness behind and get on the road to new life.

Discover a grateful heart for all that God has given you . . . on Route 66.

Materialism

It is said that when John Wesley died—Wesley, the founder of the Methodist branch of Christianity—his possessions consisted of some books, some clothes, a few coins, and a spoon with which he ate his meals— and very little else. He was like the apostle Paul, spending most of his time traveling about, preaching the Gospel. He had learned to travel lightly through this world.

All of us could benefit from a periodic look at the amount of stuff we have collected and go through the healthy spiritual process of "de-accumulation"—just to prove that it's not the stuff that owns us.

Assess what is truly valuable on the road to new life.

Discover what's important to God . . . on Route 66.

Anger

There is a Hebrew proverb that says the best way to know a man is to watch him when he is angry, suggesting there is more than one way to be angry. And while not from the Bible, that proverb is supported by Scripture.

The apostle Paul warned, "Be angry, and do not sin" (Ephesians 4:26). Anger can motivate us to correct things that are wrong in this world; but when it becomes self-serving and hurtful to others, it has gone too far. Counting to ten when you feel angry is not bad advice—you'll have time to guard against expressing yourself the wrong way.

Exercise restraint on the road to new life.

Discover God's position on anger . . . on Route 66.

Regret

Here's something you may not have thought about:
There is one kind of person on earth who never lies,
never exaggerates, never criticizes, and never brags.
Who is that person? It is the person who never
speaks. Now, I've used that impossible example to
make this point: The more we speak, the more likely
we are to say something we will regret.

That's a principle of Scripture, too. Proverbs 10:19
says that in a "multitude of words sin is not lacking."
The Book of James says to be "slow to speak."
Conquering the impulse to speak out takes self-
control, a fruit of the Holy Spirit.

Be conscientious on the road to new life.

*Discover God's gift of edifying speech . . .
on Route 66.*

Gossip

There is a story told about a man who spread malicious gossip about another person. He realized his mistake and confessed his sin to a wise old monk. To help the man see the dangers of gossip, the monk gave him a bag of feathers to scatter throughout the town on a windy day. Then the monk told the man to go back and collect all the feathers.

It is just as impossible to retrieve words we've spoken as it is to collect feathers that have been scattered by the wind. Whatever you say today, make sure your words will never need to be retrieved.

Be mindful on the road to new life.

Discover God's choice of words . . .
on Route 66.

Battle Wounds

There is an Italian proverb that says, "In warfare, the best armor is to stay out of range." While it's always best to avoid unnecessary conflicts, spiritual warfare is a different story. We have an enemy who is pursuing us—like a roaring lion. If we retreat, he advances. At some point, there is going to be a confrontation.

Fortunately, God has provided armor for Christians to wear—the "whole armor of God," as the apostle Paul called it in Ephesians 6. Many Christians today are among the walking wounded because they have not put on the very armor God provided to ensure their protection.

Equip yourself for the road to new life.

Discover the whole armor of God . . .
on Route 66.

Temptation

After the fact, some people wonder how they ever got themselves involved in a sinful situation. I have heard it said that if we will keep ourselves from the opportunity to sin, God will keep us from sin.

The New Testament says God never allows us to be tempted beyond our ability to resist, that He will provide a way of escape (1 Corinthians 10:13). The question is: Will we take the way of escape He provides? If we do, He will keep us from sin. If we don't, then we have failed to keep ourselves from the opportunity to sin. So God has a part and we have a part.

Take the road to new life.

Discover God's detours away from temptation . . . on Route 66.

Slavery to Sin

You won't find this definition in the dictionary, but I once saw "death" defined this way: "to suddenly stop sinning." That definition is biblical, of course, and makes the assumption that as long as a human being is alive, he or she has the propensity and ability to sin.

Fortunately, the Bible says it's possible to stop sinning—or at least stop having to sin—by dying spiritually instead of physically. When we die to our own self-centered desires and yield the control of our life to the Holy Spirit through faith in Christ, we are no longer slaves to sin.

Yield to God on the road to new life.

Discover His freedom from sin . . . on Route 66.

Stubborn Spirit

There's something humiliating about the word "surrender." Ever since we were kids, when the neighborhood bully put us in a headlock and refused to let us go unless we gave up, we've resisted the idea of giving in to a stronger opponent.

That may be okay in athletics and military battles, but when it comes to the spiritual life, surrender is the only way to achieve victory. God wants us to be victorious and successful in life, but He wants us to achieve victory in a way He knows is best for us. And that means first gaining victory over our stubborn pride.

Relinquish your willfulness on the road to new life.

Discover God's victory . . . on Route 66.

Speck-tating

See if you can identify with this observation:
"Have you ever noticed that anybody driving slower than you is an idiot, and anyone driving faster than you is a maniac?" Even if we don't speak quite that descriptively out loud, we all have judged others in our heart.

Jesus, of course, had a well-known corrective for our habit of viewing others as wrong and ourselves as right. He encouraged us to deal with the log in our own eye before pointing out the speck of dust in someone else's eye (Matthew 7:1-5). This is hard to do on our own, but possible with God's help.

Examine yourself on the road to new life.

Discover God's precepts . . . on Route 66.

Rage

It has been said that there was a time when a man would spend a week waiting patiently if he missed a stagecoach. But today, that same man might fly into a rage if he missed the first section of a revolving door! Same man, but two very different responses produced by cultural conditioning.

The Bible says patience is the fruit of the Holy Spirit, and the Holy Spirit was the same in the days of stagecoaches as today. It's not the Spirit or the patience that have changed—it's us. Look for an opportunity today to allow the Holy Spirit to produce patience in your life.

Keep a level head on the road to new life.

Discover God's patience . . . on Route 66.

Deep Waters

Think about two different kinds of rivers. One is a narrow, rapid, whitewater river roaring through a canyon. The other is a wide, deep river flowing silently through the flatlands. What is a prominent difference in the two rivers? The sound they make. One roars while the other is restful.

I've heard a proverb that says, "Where the river is deepest, it makes the least noise." And I have found that people are like that. The deeper the spiritual life of a person who follows Christ, the less noise he makes. Those people have a quiet, abiding trust in God: deep, wide, and restful.

Observe rest stops on the road to new life.

Discover God's depth . . . on Route 66.

Stop and Think

Someone has observed that, after thousands of years of struggling, we have advanced to the point where we have locks and bolts and alarm systems to guard us and our property while we sleep, whereas the natives in the jungle sleep in open-air huts with no doors at all.

Sometimes defining progress can be tricky. Is it progress when we are so busy that we don't have time for God in the morning or time to read our children a story at night? It's a good exercise to stop and examine our lives and ask, "Am I making progress in the things that really matter?"

Take time to prioritize on the road to new life.

Discover God's definition of progress . . .
on Route 66.

Pause

People are usually embarrassed by their picture on their passport and driver's license. They usually look more like a mug shot, don't they? In fact, I once heard this spin on an old saying: When you actually start to look like the picture on your passport, you know it's past time for a vacation!

I believe most people are overworked and "under-rested." Think of this: God's plan was for us to spend at least one-seventh of our life resting. He designated the seventh day of every week for nothing but rest. I know it's a challenge, but I encourage you to get the amount of rest God knows you need.

Pause and refresh on the road to new life.

Discover God's plan for rest . . . on Route 66.

Peace

If you are familiar with the works of Rudyard Kipling, you might recognize a modification of his words by author Jean Kerr in *Please Don't Eat the Daisies.* Kerr said, "If you can keep your head when all about you are losing theirs, it's just possible you haven't grasped the seriousness of the situation."

That may be true, but there is another possibility. It may be that you are enjoying the peace of God that the Bible promises to all who are in Christ Jesus and commit their concerns to God in prayer. Those people aren't naïve. They recognize that serious situations need to be turned over to God.

Surrender the wheel on the road to new life.

Discover God's peace . . . on Route 66.

God's Voice

Winston Churchill once wrote that "men occasionally stumble over the truth, but most of them pick themselves up and hurry off as if nothing had happened." That observation makes me wonder how many times we miss something God is trying to show us—something we want or need to know—because His still, small voice gets drowned out by the noise around us or by our own loud voices.

If there's an answer you've been searching for, no matter how big or how small, take a quiet moment today and ask God to give you ears to hear and eyes to see what He is saying.

Contemplate in quietness on the road to new life.

Discover God's still, small voice . . . on Route 66.

Dark Days

Dr. V. Raymond Edman was the fourth president of Wheaton College, a biblically-based, academically-rigorous Christian college near Chicago. Among other things, Dr. Edman is well-remembered for telling students, "Don't doubt in the darkness what God has revealed in the light."

Dark days can be emotional days, but our emotions should never cloud the light of reason and faith. Emotions are the gift of God, but they are servants of faith and reason for celebration or for caution. If you are going through a dark time right now, submit your emotions to the authority of God's Word, to His great and precious promises.

Allow God to steady your heart on the road to new life.

Discover His constancy . . . on Route 66.

Rest Assured

Imagine what the Mayflower pilgrims or Christopher Columbus must have felt the moment their homeland dropped beneath the horizon as they sailed westward. They could turn around 360 degrees on the deck of their ship and see nothing but ocean. It would have been easy to shout, "Turn around—we're going back!"

There is a thin line between fear and exhilaration. When the familiar disappears and the unfamiliar looms all around, we need the constant, reassuring presence of Christ. After all, it was He who said, "I am with you always" (Matthew 28:20). Reach out for His presence today. He is always there.

Find assurance that God is with you on the road to new life.

Discover His presence . . . on Route 66.

Understanding

Because I read a lot of books, I sometimes think how nice it would be if the author were immediately accessible to me so I could ask for help or clarification with a passage I don't quite understand. Fortunately, when I'm reading the Bible, the author is always present.

I'll be the first to admit that not everything in the Bible is crystal clear to me. But when the author, God Himself, is living inside me, I can pause and ask Him for help in understanding. When you read something in the Bible that you don't understand, just ask God to help you understand.

Ask for understanding on the road to new life.

Discover God's illumination of the Scriptures . . . on Route 66.

Beyond Control

Henry Kissinger, former Secretary of State, once remarked: "There cannot be a crisis next week. My schedule is full." Sometimes we think like that when it comes to the circumstances in our life. "Not now, God!" we say. "I just don't have time to deal with this."

And that is often God's point. He wants us to trust Him when life seems beyond our control. What better way than to allow something to come into our lives when our "schedule" is already filled. When that happens, we have to turn to Him and confess that He is able to see us through.

God is in control of the road to new life.

Discover His trustworthiness . . . on Route 66.

Count Blessings

Clichés are clichés not just because they are repeated often but because they contain a kernel of truth that makes people say, "That's really true." One such cliché is this: Things could always be worse. I know those words are small comfort at the moment when life is painful, but it's the truth—things could always be worse.

An anonymous writer said it this way: "If you can't be content with what you have received, be thankful for what you have escaped." The apostle Paul's take on it was, "In everything give thanks" (1 Thessalonians 5:18). Every moment of every day, regardless of our circumstances, we have reason to be thankful.

Acknowledge your blessings on the road to new life.

Discover God's reasons to be grateful . . . on Route 66.

Futures

The Irish playwright George Bernard Shaw said what many of us are thinking: "If all economists were laid end to end, they would not reach a conclusion." Not even the economists can agree on what the future holds.

But there is One who knows where the economy is headed, and that is God. Past, present, and future are the same to Him—He sees them all at once. Just because He knows the future doesn't mean He is going to tell us, but it does mean we can trust Him. There are no surprises in heaven.

Despite economic concerns, trust God on the road to new life.

Discover God's heavenly prospects . . . on Route 66.

Healing

Sometimes a family pet may stop eating and spend an unusual amount of time sleeping or resting. Our tendency is to make them better with remedies. But animals seem to know instinctively that the first thing, often the best thing, to do is rest and wait for healing to come naturally.

I'm not suggesting that we shouldn't take our pet to the vet—rather, that we might imitate them when we are feeling out of sorts. Instead of trying to "fix" our problem with activity, perhaps we need to rest—to grow quiet enough to hear God's voice speaking to our heart.

Find restoration on the road to new life.

Discover God's repose . . . on Route 66.

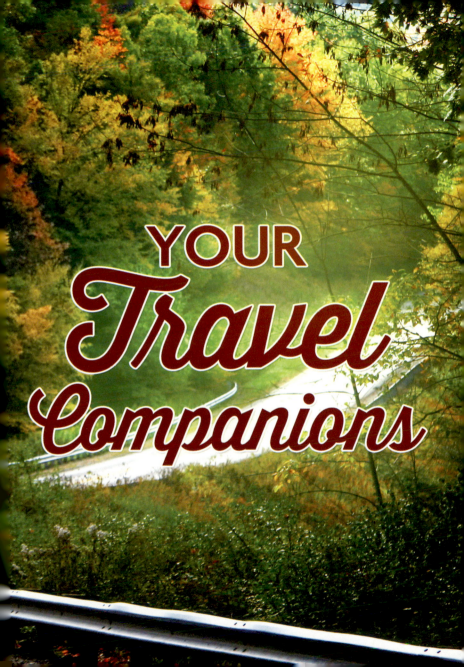

YOUR *Travel* Companions

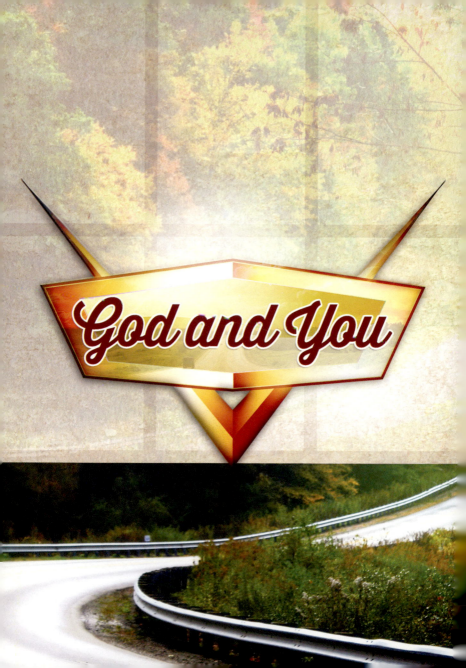

The Truth

I once read that an atheist cannot find God for the same reason a thief cannot find a policeman! Like the Russian cosmonaut who returned from space years ago saying God doesn't exist. He had looked for God outside the window of his space capsule but didn't see Him.

The Bible says exactly the opposite. Psalm 19 says the heavens declare the glory of God and show forth His handiwork for all who care to see it. And Romans 1 says that God has made His existence perfectly clear to humanity, regardless of what people who profess they cannot find Him say. Looking begins in the heart.

Look for God's handiwork on the road to new life.

Discover His truth . . . on Route 66.

Simply Profound

Famous theologian Karl Barth once lectured at an Ivy League university. After his lecture to a standing-room-only crowd, a student asked the theologian what was the most profound thought he had ever had. He said, "Jesus loves me, this I know, for the Bible tells me so."

That is a simple answer and a profound answer at the same time. Nothing could be deeper than the fact that God loves us so much that He gave His only Son so that we might have eternal life. And He gave us a written record of that fact so all the world might know of His love.

Some answers are simple on the road to new life.

Discover the depth of God's love . . .
on Route 66.

Unfailing Love

Nineteenth-century French novelist Victor Hugo wrote that "the supreme happiness of life is the conviction of being loved." And he should know. He wrote the powerful story of love and redemption, *Les Misérables*, widely considered one of history's greatest novels.

There are many people in the world who don't know they are loved by God. They may not know that God is love, or they may feel unworthy of His love. But the Bible says, "God so loved the world," which includes *everyone* in the world. So I am here to tell you today that God loves you— He always has and He always will.

God invites you to join Him on the road to new life.

Discover His unfailing love . . . on Route 66.

God's Accessibility

The American comedic actor George Jessel once said, "The human brain starts working the moment you are born and never stops until you stand up to speak in public." Trust me—I can testify to the accuracy of Mr. Jessel's observation!

As fearful as some situations in life are—and public speaking is a big one—we can be sure that God will never leave us, even if our wit and wisdom do. If you are facing a challenging assignment in life right now, be assured that God is near, waiting to give the courage and strength you need—if only you will call upon Him for help.

God is your companion on the road to new life.

Discover His accessibility . . . on Route 66.

Perpetual Presence

To improve the driving habits of American motorists, we just need enough police officers in their cruisers to follow every driver around all day. That's preposterous, of course, but you get my point. It's easy for us to be on our best behavior when we believe we are being watched.

The true test of who we are is what we do when no one is watching. But the truth is, we are never in that situation because God is always watching. He watches the hairs of our head and hears our every idle word. Let His presence be a godly influence in your life today.

Behave responsibly on the road to new life.

Discover God's perpetual presence . . . on Route 66.

Blessings

"*If you pick up a starving dog and make him* prosperous, he will not bite you. That is the principal difference between a dog and a man." With those words, Mark Twain makes a biblical point: Man is the only species on planet earth that can act ungrateful even after being blessed by God. Sometimes we think God owes us more.

But God doesn't owe us anything. Every good and perfect gift we have been given flows out of His generous love, mercy, and grace (James 1:17). Instead of biting the hand of God that has blessed us, we should be as grateful and happy as man's best friend.

Be thankful on the road to new life.

Discover God's blessings . . . on Route 66.

Initiative

Most everyone knows these words of Jesus concerning prayer: "Ask, and it will be given to you; seek, and you will find; knock, and it will be opened to you" (Matthew 7:7). But too often the idea of initiative is overlooked. God expects us to take the initiative when it comes to life. He expects us to do the asking, seeking, and knocking.

Sometimes we think that all initiative is to be left to God. After all, He is God and we are certainly not. But God has committed the responsibility for initiative to us. He expects us to move, to build, to create—and to pray.

Take initiative on the road to new life.

Discover God's responsiveness . . . on Route 66.

Religion

Looking back through history, I am always amazed at what men have done to one another in the name of religion. There have been terrible battles, wars, inquisitions, and acts of prejudice all in the name of one religion or another. It's no wonder that Jesus Christ Himself was not a huge fan of the religion of His day.

It has often been said that religion is man reaching out to God, whereas Christianity is God reaching out to man. Christianity is not a religion, but a relationship. Make sure the spiritual focus of your life is on a relationship with Christ above everything else.

Pursue the road to new life.

Discover a relationship with God . . . on Route 66.

Commitment

Do you know what happens to people who live their life in the middle of the road? They often get run over. Jesus Christ had a word for people who live in the middle of the spiritual road. He called them "lukewarm."

In chapters 2 and 3 of the Book of Revelation, the ascended Christ dictated letters to John the apostle concerning the spiritual life of seven churches in Asia Minor. One of them, the church at Laodicea, He described as being as distasteful as lukewarm water. It meant that they were apathetic and uncaring, unwilling to make a spiritual commitment to God.

Commit to the road to new life.

Discover how to be passionate for God . . . on Route 66.

Protection

One way to encourage yourself when feeling low is to think of all the adversities that might have been. We've all experienced negative events in our life, but we have been spared from many more. Perhaps we didn't make some dumb decisions we were contemplating, or maybe we were spared the consequences of some decisions we did make. In other words, things could have been worse.

The Bible tells how God kept the Israelites from encountering the warlike Philistines when they left their slavery in Egypt—protection they were unaware of at the time. Every day we should be grateful to God for how He protects us.

Be filled with gratitude on the road to new life.

Discover God's protection . . . on Route 66.

Friendship

I have heard it said that a true friend is one who laughs at your stories when they are not so good and sympathizes with your troubles even when they are not so bad. According to the Book of Proverbs, there is another thing a friend does: A true friend sticks closer than a brother. Your brother may live for you, but your friend will die for you.

Jesus called His disciples His friends and said that the greatest love a person can have is "to lay down one's life for his friends" (John 15:13). And that is exactly what Jesus did. By His death, Jesus invites you to be His friend.

Join Christ on the road to new life.

Discover His friendship . . . on Route 66.

Credit

The English philosopher Francis Bacon likened some men to the fly sitting on the axle of a chariot saying, "What a cloud of dust do I raise!" That would be like a crowing rooster taking credit for the sun coming up every morning.

Sometimes we take credit for far more than we should. In the final analysis, there is very little for which we deserve credit. The apostle Paul wrote in Romans that all things in life are of God and through God and to God—to whom all glory is due forever. That leaves precious little for us to boast about.

Boast in God on the road to new life.

Discover why He is worthy of all glory . . . on Route 66.

Priority

A quote from British author C. S. Lewis points out a flaw in how many people think about God. He wrote, "As a friend of mine said, 'We regard God as an airman regards his parachute; it's there for emergencies but he hopes he'll never have to use it.'"[2] How would you feel if your family and friends only related to you when they had an emergency?

Immanuel is a name used to describe Jesus Christ in the Bible. In the Hebrew language "Immanuel" means "God with us." It's a perfect picture of how God wants to be with us all the time—not just as a last resort.

Stay in touch on the road to new life.

Discover God's presence . . . on Route 66.

2   C. S. Lewis, *The Problem of Pain* (New York: HarperCollins, 1996), 94.

Transformation

We've all heard the expression, "You can't make a silk purse out of a sow's ear." Here's another one: "Cropping a donkey's ears will not make him a stallion." In other words, it is impossible to change the fundamental nature of something—physically or spiritually.

No matter how we shine and accessorize our sinful human nature, we cannot be transformed into someone like Jesus. That's why He said we have to be born again; it requires a brand new start. We have to become a "new creation"; we have to be *trans*-formed, not *re*-formed. And that only happens by placing our faith in Christ.

Allow God to make you "new" on the road to new life.

Discover God's transforming grace . . . on Route 66.

The Maker

It was Edith Schaeffer, I believe, the wife of the late Christian apologist Francis Schaeffer, who used large, medieval tapestries as a metaphor for the spiritual life. On the front side of a tapestry, every thread and stitch is perfect and in place. But turn the tapestry over, and you'll see what it takes to make that beautiful picture: knots, loose threads, repairs, connections, and corrected mistakes.

I like that image. God is the weaver of the tapestry of our lives. Behind the scenes, things aren't always so pretty. But every stitch, repair, and correction results in a life of great value and beauty.

You have been crafted for the road to new life.

Discover God's beautiful design . . . on Route 66.

Being Known

The famous radio comedian Fred Allen provided a good definition of a celebrity: Someone who works hard to become instantly recognized by everyone and then wears dark glasses so as not to be recognized by anyone.

Well, celebrities aren't the only people who take seriously the question of being known. Jesus Christ said that one day He would say to some people, "I never knew you; depart from Me!" It's nice to be known by other people, but eternally more important to be known by Jesus Christ. If you don't know Him, today is the day that can change.

Get to know God on the road to new life.

Discover God's desire to know you . . . on Route 66.

God is God

The novelist F. Scott Fitzgerald said that the true sign of first-rate intelligence is the ability to hold two opposite ideas at the same time without losing the ability to function.[3] Philosophers call such a position "antinomy"—two true ideas that appear to be contradictory.

For example, the Bible says that God's predestination and man's free choice are equally true—yet those two truths seem contradictory. That's because, as the prophet Isaiah wrote, our ways are not God's ways. What may seem contradictory to our mind is not contradictory to God's. We need to rest in the fact that God is God and we are not.

Find meaning on the road to new life.

Discover who God is . . . on Route 66.

3   F. Scott Fitzgerald, *The Crack-Up* (New York: New Directions, 1945), 69.

Self-Knowledge

The great British man of letters, Samuel Johnson, once observed that "almost every man wastes part of his life in attempts to display qualities which he does not possess, and to gain applause which he cannot keep."

The apostle Paul had a remedy for that kind of thinking. In Romans 12 he wrote that we should not think more highly of ourselves than we ought to think; rather, we should think of ourselves in terms of the grace and gifts God has given us. When we learn to know and value ourselves as God knows us, we have gained true self-knowledge.

Get to know yourself on the road to new life.

Discover the grace and gifts God has given you . . . on Route 66.

The Fool

A Latin proverb from many centuries ago lines up perfectly with the wisdom of Solomon in the biblical Book of Proverbs. The Latin proverb says, "Any man can make a mistake, but it takes a fool to keep making it." That reminds me of the definition I once heard of a fanatic—a person who redoubles his efforts in spite of doing the wrong thing.

A fool in the Bible is the person who pridefully persists in doing the wrong thing even after realizing he's made a mistake. A wise person, on the other hand, is the one who learns the lesson God provides and acts accordingly.

Become a student of truth on the road to new life.

Discover God's teaching . . . on Route 66.

Total Commitment

A famous Irish playwright wrote that "anybody can sympathise with the sufferings of a friend, but it requires a very fine nature . . . to sympathise with a friend's success." For the Christian, it's not a matter of either/or. We are exhorted by God to "rejoice with those who rejoice, and weep with those who weep" (Romans 12:15).

In other words, we are to act toward others just like we would act toward ourselves. Or, in the words of the Golden Rule, we are to treat others like we would want to be treated. Sympathy when needed and rejoicing when expected. That means being totally committed to others.

Be committed to helping others on the road to new life.

Discover God's family ties . . . on Route 66.

Loyal-Love

Most Christians are familiar with agape, the most important word for love in the New Testament. But there is an equally important word used in the Old Testament to describe God's love, and that is the Hebrew word *hesed,* meaning "loyal-love." Throughout the Old Testament, God affirmed His loyal-love toward the nation of Israel.

Loyalty doesn't mean you always agree, but it does mean you keep your promises and stand by your word. We know God is loyal to us, but do those we love know that we are loyal to them? Take the opportunity to communicate and demonstrate your loyal-love to those in your life.

Be steadfast on the road to new life.

Discover God's loyal-love . . . on Route 66.

Marriage

Author and teacher Emerson Eggerichs, in the title of his popular book on marriage, has summed up the essence of this divine institution with two biblical words: love and respect. As complicated as marriage can seem, it really boils down to two simple ideas.

Husbands are to love their wives like Christ loves the Church, and wives are to respect their husbands like the Church respects and honors her Lord (Ephesians 5:22-33). The more husbands love, the more wives respect. And the more wives respect, the more husbands love. But who goes first? Who makes the first move? You do—believing that God will honor His Word.

Display love and respect on the road to new life.

Discover God's design for marriage . . . on Route 66.

Arguments

I have heard it said that there are two sides to every argument, and they're usually married to each other. While that observation raises a smile, there is a wealth of wisdom in it. God created the first woman because the first man was incomplete; he was only one "side" of the argument.

Like all couples, my wife and I have found ourselves on opposite sides of a discussion many times. But we have also learned that if we remove the emotion from the moment, we find our opposite views can lead us to a solution neither of us would have discovered alone.

Seek unity and understanding on the road to new life.

Discover God's plan for matrimony . . . on Route 66.

Tears

We hear a lot today about alternative forms of energy, including waterpower. But one early twentieth-century playwright was way ahead of the rest of us. He said that the most efficient and effective source of waterpower in the world is a woman's tears.

As a husband and father, I have to agree. If I see a tear in my wife or daughter's eye, I'm putty in their hand. And willingly so. I have learned that the sensitive spirit God created in women is often a barometer to which I should pay close attention. Men, let's thank God for a woman's tears.

Be perceptive on the road to new life.

Discover God's gift of a woman's sensitivity . . . on Route 66.

Communication

There is an ancient Chinese proverb that says, "Married couples who love each other tell each other a thousand things without talking." They do it, of course, with the nonverbal use of their eyes, their touch, their body language, and their presence or their absence. Experts tell us that more is said nonverbally between lovers than verbally. That's why email, Tweets, and text messages can be dangerous—because they omit the nonverbal dimensions of communication.

It is also why God gave us a written Word, the Bible, and a living Word, Jesus Christ—that we would get the full impact of what He is saying to us.

Communicate on the road to new life.

Discover what God has to say . . . on Route 66.

Intimacy

One day a father was gently explaining the "facts of life" to his young son after the little boy had asked where babies come from. The little boy listened with rapt attention and wide eyes. His father concluded and asked his son if he had any questions. The little boy had just one: "Do you think God knows about this?"

In a culture in which sex has become a commercial commodity, it's easy to forget that it is a beautiful part of God's creation—something He designed both for procreation and pleasure within marriage. Like all things, it should be enjoyed for His glory.

You were designed for one another on the road to new life.

Discover God's beautiful gifts . . . on Route 66.

Conflict Resolution

The well-known comedienne Phyllis Diller offered some advice that began constructively. "Never go to bed mad," she began. But then she said, "Instead, stay up and fight." Well, it is fortunate that Ms. Diller didn't abandon comedy and go into counseling!

Better advice is found in Paul's letter to the Ephesians where he began the same way: "Do not let the sun go down on your anger," Paul wrote—period. In other words, don't go to bed mad and don't stay up and fight. Instead, stay up and resolve your anger through love and forgiveness. That's a sure prescription for a good night's sleep.

Put problems to rest on the road to new life.

Discover God's remedy for conflict resolution . . . on Route 66.

Receptiveness

We can all agree that wisdom is an essential ingredient for making God-honoring decisions. As experienced adults, it is important that we pass our knowledge and understanding on to the younger generation and equip them to make their own decisions. While your words may often fall on deaf ears, repetition and gentleness are invaluable.

But the Bible also has very positive things to say about *receiving* wise advice. "A wise man *will* hear and increase learning, and a man of understanding will attain wise counsel" (Proverbs 1:5). Regardless of our age, all of us can benefit from counselors—whether they are parents, pastors, or a good friend. Be open to receiving a word of advice today. It might turn out to be heaven-sent.

Heed wise direction on the road to new life.

Discover God's advice . . . about advice . . . on Route 66.

Responsibility

Here's good advice for all parents and grandparents from Abigail Van Buren, the iconic "Dear Abby" columnist: "If you want children [or grandchildren] to keep their feet on the ground, put some responsibility on their shoulders." I like that! Sometimes we forget that God created us to be responsible people— and that includes children. And it takes having responsibility to learn to be responsible.

The first thing God gave Adam and Eve was responsibility. He put them in charge of His creation—everything He had made. Of course, I would suggest a slightly smaller responsibility for your children. They'll feel great when they've succeeded and so will you.

Be a dynamic parent on the road to new life.

Discover God's plan for raising great kids . . . on Route 66.

Healthy Influences

Here are a couple of observations about television, the implications of which are self-evident. British talk-show host David Frost said, "Television is an invention that permits you to be entertained in your living room by people you would never invite into your home." And the late comedienne Erma Bombeck said, "In general, my children refused to eat anything that hadn't danced on television."

The lessons there are obvious—especially with regard to our children. Watching television is an invitation to be influenced by whatever we see. As stewards of the grace of God, we need to choose our influences wisely. And turn off the unhealthy ones.

Use discernment on the road to new life.

Discover God's influence . . . on Route 66.

Ready? Parenting

President Teddy Roosevelt had six children. Regarding his sixteen-year-old daughter, Alice, he once said, "I can either be President of the United States or I can control Alice. I cannot do both." I imagine every parent has felt that way at times.

There's no question that parenting is a full-time job. Fortunately, we have a full-time helper—God's Holy Spirit. He is the One who promises to give us love, joy, peace, patience, and everything else we need to be good parents. Before you decide to quit your job of raising your teenager, ask God's Spirit to give you the help you need.

Show loving devotion on the road to new life.

Discover God's resources for parents . . . on Route 66.

Teenagers

I once read that God made it easier for parents to release their children into the world by inventing the teen years. Yes, it's true—adolescence is a challenging time for children and parents alike. But so is childbirth! And adolescence for teens is like being born into a strange new world of emotions and expectations.

Believe it or not, Jesus was a teenager once. In the Gospel of Luke we get a quick glimpse of what He was like at age twelve—growing in wisdom and stature. That's what all parents want for their teens—and we parents can help by being their biggest encouragers.

Help your kids grow on the road to new life.

Discover God's way to parent . . . on Route 66.

Opportunity Knocking

You've probably heard popular sayings about opportunity, like this one: Opportunity knocks on the door, but we still have to get up to answer it. And this one: The sign on the door of opportunity reads "Push." And this one: Opportunities are seldom labeled as such.

There's a lot of wisdom in those sayings. But there is a greater piece of wisdom about opportunity for the Christian: God oversees the events of our lives. He puts opportunities before us every day that we may miss if we're not careful—even if it's just the opportunity to speak a word of encouragement to a family member or friend.

Search for opportune moments on the road to new life.

Discover God's well-timed open doors of opportunity . . . on Route 66.

Strength

If you have ever looked closely at a piece of rope— one that is thick enough to support a heavy weight— you know it is made up of hundreds of tiny threads that are wound together to form a single rope. Even the giant steel cables that hold up suspension bridges are made up of tiny steel threads.

It's no wonder then that Solomon wrote in Ecclesiastes that a threefold cord is not quickly broken. He was talking about people, of course. While a single individual can be overpowered, a group of three together is much, much stronger—for many, many reasons.

Find support on the road to new life.

*Discover strength in godly friends . . .
on Route 66.*

Friends

An English poet of the Middle Ages, Geoffrey Chaucer, won his reputation with advice like this: "My son," he wrote, "keep well thy tongue, and keep thy friend." That was true in the Middle Ages and is still true today. Gossip destroys friendships quicker than anything.

That was also true some twenty-five hundred years before Chaucer. Twice in the Book of Proverbs we read that a whisperer, or a person who repeats a matter, is a person who separates the best of friends. If you have a friend and you want to keep him or her, take the advice of Chaucer and Solomon.

"Keep well thy tongue" on the road to new life.

Discover God's way to be a trusted friend . . . on Route 66.

Peer Pressure

Not many cooks use them today; but when I was young, "pressure cookers" were the rage. Add water, seal the lid, turn up the heat, and pressure in the pot did the rest. Life is full of pressures today, and none is more intense than peer pressure.

If we dismiss peer pressure as a junior high school thing, something that doesn't affect us, we're in denial. Everybody cares what others think. And that can even be a good thing! Part of managing peer pressure is learning to choose wise friends. The Bible's Book of Proverbs is full of good ideas on that subject.

Are you in good company on the road to new life?

Discover God's thoughts on friendship . . . on Route 66.

Honesty

There's an interesting verse about flattery in the Book of Proverbs. It says, "A man who flatters his neighbor spreads a net for his feet." But it isn't clear whose feet are about to get caught in the trap. Is the person doing the flattering or the person receiving the flattery about to be trapped?

In a strict sense, I think the verse says that the person being flattered is the one in danger because he is being seduced without knowing it. But the person who speaks flattering words is also in danger. When his flattery is discovered, he will have lost a friend.

False flattery is a dead end on the road to new life.

Discover God's honest ways of speaking . . . on Route 66.

Peaceable Living

Benjamin Franklin came up with the idea of street lamps in Philadelphia. He said that if everyone put a lamp in front of his own house, then the whole street would be illuminated at night. A corollary idea is this: If everyone sweeps in front of his door, the whole street will be clean.

None of us can do everything, but all of us can do our part. The apostle Paul expressed that idea when he wrote, "As much as depends on you, live peaceably with all men" (Romans 12:18). If every person chooses to live in peace, then the whole family, church, or community will live in peace.

Encourage harmony on the road to new life.

Discover God's plan for peaceable living . . . on Route 66.

Strong Connections

I once read a funny observation about mountain climbers that offers some real wisdom for life. It said that mountain climbers always rope themselves together to prevent the fearful ones from turning and going home. Life, like mountain climbing, can definitely be scary at times; and it helps to be roped together with some folks who are stronger.

The New Testament exhorts Christians to gather together in groups to encourage one another in love and good works—and, yes, to hang in there when the going gets tough. If you're not part of a community of fellow Christians who have a strong spiritual rope, you should be.

Get connected on the road to new life.

Discover God's reasons for community . . . on Route 66.

Heart Trouble

There is an old German proverb that says, "When a dove begins to associate with crows, its feathers remain white but its heart grows black." The point is not to disparage the crows of the world, but to say that changes can happen on the inside even when things look normal on the outside.

There are verses in the Bible that warn about the dangers of intimate association with those who do not share our spiritual values. On the other hand, we are called to befriend all who need the love of God, being careful to keep our hearts pure and our values in place.

Be steadfast in your faith on the road to new life.

Discover God's guidelines for close friendships . . . on Route 66.

Do You Understand?

Henny Youngman, the king of the one-liners, used to say that his mother-in-law was so concerned with neatness that she spread out a newspaper under the cuckoo clock—just in case.

All of us know people who are a challenge to live with, and we are sometimes a challenge ourselves. So what do we do in those situations? The Bible has some very helpful advice on this subject. It says we ought to extend the same understanding and forgiveness to others that God extends to us. After all, if He can extend grace to us, we ought to be able to extend that same grace to others.

Practice understanding and forgiveness on the road to new life.

Discover God's extension of grace . . . on Route 66.

Part of Life

On September 3, 2007, according to the U.S. Census Bureau, there were 6.6 billion people in the world. And the population of the United States on that day was 302.7 million. You and I will never meet, much less know, the vast majority of those people.

But God has chosen a few and made them part of our lives. And one of the reasons is so we might show them His love, that we might be His hands reaching out to touch their needs. Think about the people God has put in your life, and touch them with His love today.

Be His hands on the road to new life.

Discover God's love for others . . .
on Route 66.

Union of Forgivers

The late Ruth Bell Graham, wife of evangelist Billy Graham, said this about marriage: "A good marriage is the union of two forgivers." On that note, let me ask this: When was the last time you quietly and consciously forgave your spouse?—or a good friend if you're not married?

If it's been a long time, something's wrong. You know your spouse isn't perfect, so you've had plenty of opportunities to forgive. And forgiving usually involves sacrifice, which means pain, so you're not likely to forget quickly. Stay alert today—watch for an opportunity to forgive the person you love most.

Forgive your loved ones on the road to new life.

Discover God's way to forgive . . . on Route 66.

Differences

Humorist Dave Barry once wrote about the differences between men and women: "What Women Want: To be loved, to be listened to, to be desired, to be respected, to be needed, to be trusted, and sometimes, just to be held. What Men Want: Tickets for the World Series."

He might be off on the details, but the point is well made: We're all different. God would add this point: We are uniquely made for a purpose. As we attempt to understand and appreciate one another's differences, we affirm and honor each other. Welcome the differences!

Honor one another on the road to new life.

Discover God's unique purpose for man and woman . . . on Route 66.

Friendly Wounds

Why is the phrase "It's none of my business . . ." always followed by the word "but"? If you've ever had someone approach you and say, "You know, it's none of my business"—you know what the next word is going to be. We use that phrase because we don't think we have the right to interfere in others' lives.

But there are some times when interference is absolutely necessary—like when we see someone involved in a dangerous or hurtful lifestyle. The Bible says, "Faithful are the wounds of a friend" (Proverbs 27:6). Sometimes we need to love others enough to intervene.

Be a faithful friend on the road to new life.

Discover God's timing for intervention . . . on Route 66.

Mirror

Someone has said that a true friend is the best kind of mirror. A true friend is one who is willing to describe your blemishes as well as your highlights. A true friend is honest—insofar as he is able to describe what he sees.

But there is actually a better kind of mirror to use when we want to see who we are beneath the surface. And that is the Word of God. When we read the Bible, we see what God expects us to be; and the Holy Spirit shows us who we really are in comparison to that.

Take a look at your reflection on the road to new life.

Discover how God sees you . . . on Route 66.

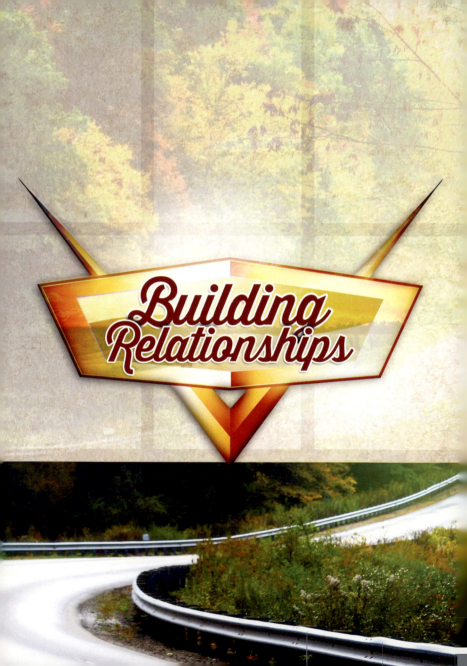

Conversation Starters

An American comedic actress, Lisa Kirk, made a wise observation about what people talk about. She said gossips talk about other people, bores talk about themselves, and a brilliant conversationalist is a person who talks to you about you! Of course, we think anyone is brilliant who wants to talk about us—but her point is well made for another reason.

A fundamental principle in the New Testament is the idea of being more concerned about others than we are about ourselves. And one way we do that is by taking a genuine interest in others' lives. And conversation is a great place to begin.

Be a person who cares about others on the road to new life.

Discover God's plan for relating to others . . . on Route 66.

Promises

Bernard Baruch was a financial investor who became wealthy and then became an economic advisor to several U.S. presidents, including Woodrow Wilson, Franklin Roosevelt, and others. His exposure to the financial and political worlds led him to this conclusion: "Vote for the man who promises least. He'll be the least disappointing."

That pessimistic outlook on politicians reminds me of something Jesus said: "Let your 'Yes' be 'Yes,' and your 'No,' 'No'" (Matthew 5:37). In other words, say what you mean and mean what you say. If you make promises, keep them. If you have given your word to someone but have yet to fulfill that promise, let your yes become yes—today.

Be reliable on the road to new life.

Discover God's promises . . . on Route 66.

Patience

A hundred years ago, patience meant waiting for a week while the mail traveled cross-country by train. Today, patience means waiting fifteen seconds when our email arrives slowly due to congestion on the Internet. We've made great strides in technology, but our advances haven't eliminated the need for patience.

This is especially true of relationships. I am learning to be patient with other people by remembering they have to be patient with me. And I'm helped by the Bible's reminder that God is patient with us all. I don't know how He does it—which makes me want to know Him better.

Make strides in patience on the road to new life.

Discover the nature of God . . . on Route 66.

Pleasing

Herbert Swope won the first Pulitzer Prize for newspaper reporting in 1917. Besides being remembered for his journalistic talents, he is also remembered for this observation: "I cannot give you the formula for success," he said, "but I can give the formula for failure, which is, try to please everybody all the time."

The apostle Paul put this idea another way. His one goal in life was to please the Lord Jesus Christ—all the time. My own contribution to this idea is that the more we please Christ, the more we please those around us when it comes to kindness, goodness, patience, and love.

It is impossible to please everyone on the road to new life.

Discover how to please God . . . on Route 66.

Truth in Love

It has been well said that deception has its own wardrobes, but truth needs no covering but love. Many people have noted through the years that the advantage of telling the truth is never having to remember what you told or to whom. Speaking the truth means saying the same thing every time.

But that doesn't mean saying everything that is true in every situation. The apostle Paul noted that truth must always be clothed in love, that truth must always be used to edify and encourage, never embarrassing or tearing down. Two things to do today: speak the truth and speak the truth in love.

Determine to speak lovingly on the road to new life.

Discover God's encouraging truth . . .
on Route 66.

Open Arms

Here is something I've discovered through the years when talking with people: There's the *good* reason, and then there's the *real* reason. Sometimes people are afraid to admit the real reason for their actions or fears. They are afraid of what others might think, afraid they will be made fun of.

The Book of Proverbs says that "the purposes of a man's heart are deep waters, but a man of understanding draws them out" (Proverbs 20:5, NIV 1984). Drawing out the real reasons from a hesitant heart takes love, tenderness, and patience. But it can be done. God may want to use you this week to help someone open his heart.

Extend kindness on the road to new life.

Discover God's ways to help others . . . on Route 66.

Keeping Score

When NBA basketball player Stacy King was a rookie on the Chicago Bulls team, he scored one point in a game in which the famous Michael Jordan scored sixty-nine points. After the game he said, "I'll always remember this game as the one in which Michael Jordan and I combined to score seventy points!"

Well, you can't argue with his math. And you can't argue with his philosophy either. In a team sport, it doesn't matter who gets the credit. Likewise, as Christians, we don't serve one another to get credit but to build up and strengthen the entire body of Christ.

Be humble on the road to new life.

Discover God's opportunities for service . . . on Route 66.

Value

Sir Thomas Browne was a seventeenth-century British author who made a practical observation. He wrote that "rough diamonds may sometimes be mistaken for worthless pebbles." I am sure that has happened in the field where inexperienced prospectors are searching for precious metals. But it also happens in relationships.

God hasn't created any "worthless pebbles" when it comes to people—only "diamonds in the rough" just waiting to break through and reveal their true value. Don't make the mistake of overlooking your own, or someone else's, true value in God's sight.

Don't discount yourself or others on the road to new life.

Discover God's definition of worth . . . on Route 66.

Love Thy Neighbor

G. K. Chesterton was a wry British writer who combined humor with sharp insights on culture and Christianity. Take these words, for example: "The Bible tells us to love our neighbors," he wrote, "and also to love our enemies; probably because they are generally the same people."

So, whether you get along well with your neighbors or not, the Christian's responsibility is to love them. Think for a moment about your neighbors—needs they might have today that you might be able to meet. And then demonstrate Christ's love for your neighbor by being the one to meet that need.

Care for others on the road to new life.

Discover God's love for your neighbors . . . on Route 66.

Needs

Charles Schulz, the creator of the famous Peanuts cartoons, had an interesting perspective on jogging for exercise. He said that while jogging is very good for our body, jogging is also good for the ground. "Jogging makes the ground feel needed," he said. He makes an interesting point.

When was the last time you asked someone to help you with a task even though you were entirely capable of doing it alone? Feeling needed is important. Technically, God doesn't need us, yet He asks us to help Him by serving others and by spreading the Gospel. And we can do the same with others.

Fulfill the needs of others on the road to new life.

Discover how you can be used of God . . . on Route 66.

Peace of Mind

J. P. McEvoy was a syndicated cartoonist who is credited with this pithy saying: "Peace of mind is better than giving them 'a piece of your mind.'" It's hard to do both at the same time: have peace of mind yourself while giving someone a piece of your mind.

The Bible puts the responsibility for living in peace squarely on our shoulders. The Book of Hebrews says to pursue peace with all, and Romans says, insofar as it depends on us, to make every effort to live at peace with others. In other words, the lack of peace between ourselves and others should never be our fault.

Pursue peace on the road to new life.

Discover God's accord and goodwill with others . . . on Route 66.

Keep Secrets

The French have a saying that puts the blame squarely where it belongs. They say, "When a secret is revealed, it is the fault of the man who confided it." Did you get that? If someone tells one of your secrets, don't blame the person who spilled the beans. Blame yourself.

The Bible also has a saying about secrets. Proverbs 25:9 says, "Debate your case with your neighbor, and do not disclose the secret to another." That is, if you have something important to say, tell it only to the person it involves and no one else. Do not tell sensitive information to insensitive people.

Be discreet on the road to new life.

Discover God's rules for relationships . . . on Route 66.

Divine Appointments

Several times in the Old Testament, individuals like Abraham, Balaam, and Gideon were visited by angels. The strange thing is that, at first, the humans didn't realize they were speaking with angelic beings. The writer to the Hebrews no doubt had those experiences in mind when he told his readers to be hospitable to strangers because it might be an angel at the door.

No one would deny hospitality or courtesy to an angel, yet we are tempted to do so to people when we are rushed or preoccupied. That verse—Hebrews 13:2—should make us see every encounter as a divine appointment.

Treat others with hospitality on the road to new life.

Discover God's divine appointments . . . on Route 66.

Integrity

I have read that buying a car, new or used, ranks near the top of consumers' most feared experiences. Maybe it's negotiating the price or fear of hidden defects that makes people wary. Regardless of the kind of transaction, everybody is looking for trust.

Truth is like money. When we give and receive truth, trust is established. We give money to purchase a product, and we give truth to purchase trust. To the degree that we don't tell the whole truth, the trust factor is diminished. When you interact with people today, do everything you can to build the trust factor. Where trust abounds, fear is gone.

Display sincerity and candor on the road to new life.

*Discover God's trustworthiness . . .
on Route 66.*

Thinking the Best

If you are or have been the parent of young boys, you may agree with this quip: Just because you haven't heard anything from your young son during the last hour doesn't mean he's up to some kind of mischief . . . It could be he's sleeping!

To be fair, mischief and sleeping aren't the *only* things young boys do. But that bit of humor illustrates how quickly we jump to negative conclusions about people or situations without knowing the facts. There is nothing loving about that. The apostle Paul said that true love "thinks no evil" (1 Corinthians 13:4-6). It believes and hopes for the best in every situation.

Think positively on the road to new life.

Discover God's way of thinking . . . on Route 66.

Open-Mindedness

I have heard it said that people never really agree with opinions expressed by others. They only agree with their own opinion when it happens to be expressed by another person. That's convicting—I hope I'm more open-minded than that.

I won't waver on what the Bible says; but in other matters, I hope I'll always value the wisdom and opinions of others. Such an attitude begins with what James wrote in his letter: "Be quick to hear" (James 1:19). Be willing to listen to others. If I believe God is at work in other people, then I believe He can speak to me through them.

Endeavor to keep an open mind on the road to new life.

Discover God's ways to learn and grow . . . *on Route 66.*

Listen

Someone once observed that many people are easily entertained—all you have to do is sit down and listen to them talk. I think there is a positive insight in that observation. There are many people in our world who would benefit from a listening ear, not for entertainment, but for encouragement.

Many times in the New Testament we are told to serve one another, love one another, and encourage one another. And it may be that the simplest way to do that is to listen to one another with a compassionate heart. Just as God listens to us, we should likewise listen to each other.

Lend a listening ear on the road to new life.

Discover God's attentiveness . . . on Route 66.

Common Denominator

The best way to think about community is to think about the word that community is built on—the word "common." A community is made up of people who have things in common. At the very least, they have in common the place where they live. But community goes deeper than geography.

Too often, Christians withdraw from their communities because they think they have nothing in common with those who believe differently. But Jesus didn't withdraw. He lived in the midst of the people with whom He shared humanity—life's most common denominator—and who needed what He came to give.

You have something in common with everyone on the road to new life.

Discover God's view of community . . . on Route 66.

Mercy

The great sixteenth-century reformer, Martin Luther, wrote that serving God is "nothing else than to show mercy to our neighbor. For it is our neighbor who needs our service; God in heaven needs it not." I think Luther would agree that serving our neighbor is a good way to serve our God.

And what is mercy? It is withholding a response of judgment even when it is deserved. That's why the Bible says God shows us mercy by forgiving us instead of judging us. And who is our neighbor? Anyone who needs the mercy that we are in a position to give.

Withhold judgment on the road to new life.

Discover God's mercy . . . on Route 66.

Encouragement

Imagine this: You're hiking in a desert area with plenty of supplies and you come across a person who has been lost for days and is dying of thirst. Your gift of water saves his life. That would be a wonderful feeling, would it not? Well, you and I can have that feeling every day by following the words of Proverbs 25:25: "Like cold water to a weary soul is good news from a distant land" (NIV 1984).

A word of good news, a word of encouragement, is sometimes all it takes to revive a weary soul— especially if it's the Good News of how God loves him or her.

Encourage others on the road to new life.

Discover God's Good News . . . on Route 66.

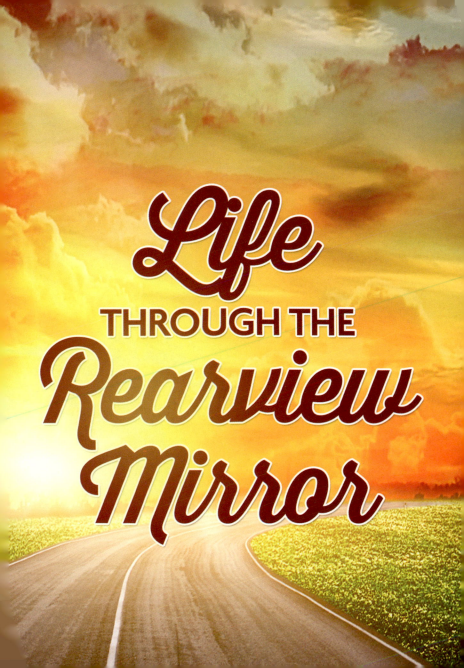

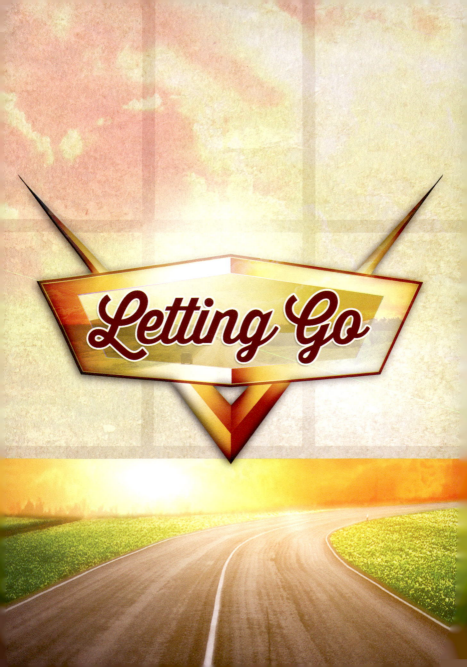

Past Sin

English novelist William Thackeray observed that it is much easier to die for one's faith than it is to live up to it. All serious Christians—like the apostle Peter—know this to be true. Peter gladly died for his Savior as a martyr in Rome, but only after having tasted the bitter tears of his own unfaithfulness when he denied even knowing Jesus.

How I thank God for forgiveness! All who have failed to live up to their professions of faith should turn to God for the forgiveness He promises to all who confess their sins. If that is you, ask for His forgiveness today.

Begin anew on the road to new life.

Discover God's forgiveness . . . on Route 66.

Painful Memories

When I was growing up, personal diaries were popular. Some even had clasps that required a key to open them to safeguard the secrets within. One Irish writer said that "memory . . . is the diary that we all carry about with us."

Everyone's memory is filled with secrets—some of which we'd like to forget. Perhaps we've sinned against God or hurt another person—or done something for which we can't forgive ourselves. Why not exchange those painful memories for the memories of reconciliation and forgiveness. God and others will forgive you, and you can forgive yourself.

Let go of troublesome memories on the road to new life.

Discover God's path to reconciliation . . . on Route 66.

Prodigal Living

A village in France received an unexpected gift.
One of its residents left home after World War II,
went to Australia, and made a fortune. He had no
heirs, so he left his entire estate—1.4 million Euros—
to his former village to be used for the needy.

Not all young men who leave home fare so well. The
Bible tells of one who squandered a fortune, instead
of making a fortune, and returned home shortly
thereafter in disgrace. This prodigal had a gracious
father and was welcomed with open arms. That father
shows how God welcomes us regardless of what we've
done with our lives.

Find acceptance on the road to new life.

Discover God's open arms . . . on Route 66.

Guilt

The writer Ogden Nash said, "There is only one way to achieve happiness on this terrestrial ball. And that is to have either a clear conscience or none at all." That is better poetry than it is theology.

The Bible says that, like it or not, everyone has a conscience. Since we can't live without a conscience, the only path to happiness is to live with a clear one. One of the Old Testament psalmists put it this way: "Blessed is the man whose sin the LORD does not count against him and in whose spirit is no deceit" (Psalm 32:2, NIV 1984). In other words, "How blessed is the man who has been cleansed of his guilt!" I have been *there* and done *that,* and agree: There's no conscience like a clean conscience!

Be released from guilt on the road to new life.

Discover God's solution for remorse . . . on Route 66.

Failures

The Watergate scandal resulted not only in the resignation of President Nixon but in the prosecution of a number of his close advisors. It became a benchmark for how seemingly good people can be caught up in doing bad things. Billy Graham made the observation about the scandal saying, "Everybody has a little bit of Watergate in him."

What he meant by that comment is that we all have potential to do wrong because of our sinful nature. It's what the Bible calls sin—and it's why God sent Jesus Christ into the world: to pay the price for our sinfulness.

Receive forgiveness on the road to new life.

Discover God's propitiation for sin . . . on Route 66.

Concealed Sin

After a Sunday school teacher had concluded her lesson, she asked the children, "What must we do before we can receive forgiveness for sin?" The room was quiet—then a little boy yelled out, "Sin!"

Well, technically he was right. We have to sin before we can be forgiven. But the Bible assumes what we also know personally, that all have sinned. It moves on and says that if we confess our sins, God is faithful and just to forgive us and cleanse us from all unrighteousness. If you have sinned but haven't confessed it to God, perhaps now would be a good time to receive His forgiveness.

Acknowledge sin on the road to new life.

Discover God's mercy . . . on Route 66.

Bondage

I read about a burglar who was surprised by a homeowner while robbing a house in Belgium. The thief ran out the back door of the house, climbed up a brick wall at the back of the property, and dropped down the other side—only to discover that he had landed in the yard of the local prison.

Running from our sins always has that effect—we land in the prison of guilt from which there is no escape without confession and forgiveness. If you are in the prison of guilt, find God's forgiveness today. It is the only door to the freedom you seek.

Don't run from your sin on the road to new life.

Discover deliverance through Christ . . . on Route 66.

Denial

I have heard it said that the most noble way for a man to be right is for a man to admit when he is wrong. That's a tough call for any of us—nobody likes to say, "I was wrong. Would you please forgive me?" Our pride is our biggest enemy.

The word "confess" in the New Testament is interesting. It literally means "to say the same as." So when we confess our sins to God, we are agreeing with Him about the fact that we were wrong. That doesn't make it easy—but it does mean He already knows what we did and is ready to forgive.

Embark on the road to new life.

Discover God's loving embrace . . .
on Route 66.

Make Amends

If you are like me, you've experienced buyer's remorse a time or two in life. We shop, pray, and then lay our money down—and before we get home, we feel guilty. Buyer's remorse is a bad feeling, but not nearly as bad as sinner's remorse.

Taking something back to a store is a lot easier than taking something back that we've said or done. Once our words or actions have hurt another person, it is hard to undo the damage. But there is an upside to remorse: It compels us to make amends. The Bible says God is ready to forgive, and so are most people, if we will ask.

Make amends on the road to new life.

Discover God's redemption . . . on Route 66.

Revenge

The Spanish have a wise saying about seeking revenge: "No revenge is more honorable than the revenge not taken." History and Hollywood tell us the opposite: that the most honorable revenge is the one taken in full, and then some! But the Spanish got this one right—as far as God is concerned.

In the New Testament, the apostle Paul gives us God's perspective when he says, "Do not take revenge . . . for it is written: 'It is mine to avenge; I will repay,' says the Lord" (Romans 12:19, NIV 1984). Instead of seeking revenge, Paul says, live at peace with everyone—even those who have hurt us.

Choose righteousness over wrath on the road to new life.

Discover God's justice . . . on Route 66.

Bygone Burdens

Seneca, the Roman orator and writer, had this touching perspective on the troubles we face in our lives. He said, "The things that are hardest to bear are sweetest to remember." I'm not sure what led Seneca to that conclusion, but I definitely know what leads me to agree with Him.

The most challenging time in my life was dealing with a life-threatening illness that God graciously brought me through. And I can honestly say, looking back, that it was the deepest period of spiritual growth in my life. It was another confirmation that God causes all things to work together for good to those who love Him (Romans 8:28).

Grow through past experiences on the road to new life.

Discover God's goodness in every circumstance . . . on Route 66.

Remorse

The famous German philosopher Friedrich Nietzsche once observed that there is an advantage to having a bad memory. The advantage is being able to have a first-time experience of joy or surprise over and over! There may be something to that in the mental realm—and there definitely is in the spiritual realm.

The prophet Jeremiah wrote that God's mercy and compassion are "new every morning" (Lamentations 3:22-23). Every day brings with it a fresh encounter with God's everlasting love and never-ending patience. Just when we think God has grown tired of our sin or weakness, He reveals His mercy anew— every morning—like a first-time gift!

Experience God's mercy on the road to new life.

Discover His readiness to forgive and redeem . . . on Route 66.

Debt

A mother once overheard her little boy explaining the basics of Christian theology to his little sister. "You see," he said, "it was Jesus' job to die for our sins, and it's our job to sin." Well, he sort of got it right. Sinning is definitely what we do; it comes naturally to us.

And it was definitely Jesus' "job"—or His mission, if you will—to come to earth to die for the sins we commit. We can commit the sins—no problem there—but we don't seem to be able to pay for them. Thankfully, Jesus is able to do what we cannot.

Find grace along the road to new life.

Discover God's divine deliverance . . . on Route 66.

Mistakes

In a letter written to a friend a year before he died, Thomas Jefferson included a list of ten practical guidelines for living. Number three said, "Never spend your money before you have it." If Jefferson had written this rule near the beginning of his life, we might have questioned his sincerity since his lavish spending left him deeply in debt when he died. But since it was written near the end, let's hope he was saying, "Learn from my mistakes."

The Book of Proverbs would agree. A wise man is one who learns from his errors and doesn't repeat them throughout life.

Press forward on the road to new life.

Discover God's instruction . . . on Route 66.

Acceptance

A former ice hockey player talked about the humiliation associated with being a goalie on your home ice. When you make a mistake, that is, when the other team scores, a red light goes on, a horn blares, and thousands of people start booing—all because you failed at your job.

What if every mistake we made in life were recognized with that kind of public display? It wouldn't be long before we would try to cover up all our mistakes, not to mention our sins. Thankfully, the Bible invites us to come to God just as we are—mistakes, sins, and all.

There will be times when we fail on the road to new life.

Discover God's acceptance and love . . .
on Route 66.

Obedience

A Greek proverb says, "Learn to obey before you command." There was a king in the Old Testament whose ability to command—his kingship—was taken from him by God because he had not learned to obey. God gave Saul a clear task to perform which he failed to carry out. He could not obey and so proved he was unqualified to command.

Almost everyone functions at some level of command. Parents, employers, bosses, teachers, coaches, government officials—almost everybody commands somebody. The more obedient we are to those over us—starting with God—the better we will be at leading those under us.

Let God shape you into a leader on the road to new life.

Discover God's reasons for obedience . . . on Route 66.

Focus

Today in this country, we don't often see farmers plowing their fields using animals for power—horses or oxen. But in Jesus' day it was common. And Jesus used the image of the plowman to make an important spiritual point. He said, "No one, having put his hand to the plow, and looking back, is fit for the kingdom of God" (Luke 9:62).

To keep his furrow straight, the plowman is always looking forward so the present furrow is right next to the previous one. Jesus was saying, "Don't doubt your commitment to follow Me. Don't look back. Don't be indecisive. Keep looking ahead."

Concentrate on the road to new life.

Discover God's reasons to stay focused on Christ . . . on Route 66.

Sanctification

It has been said that anyone who believes that practice makes perfect doesn't have a child taking piano or violin lessons. It's not true that practice makes perfect, but it is true that practice makes progress toward perfection—even if we never achieve it.

The Bible has a big word to describe making progress in the Christian life: *sanctification.* In short, it means making progress in becoming more like Jesus, which Romans 8:29 says is God's ultimate goal for us. Sanctification in this life is an ongoing process of progress toward perfection—perfection we will only achieve when we find ourselves in the presence of Christ Himself.

Continue to grow in your faith on the road to new life.

Discover God's path to perfection . . . on Route 66.

God's Best

Take note of this worthwhile observation: "Things seem to turn out best for those who make the best of the way things turn out."

You may not realize it at first, but there is a biblical truth buried in there. Besides being optimistic, it reminds us that God causes all things to work together for good to those who love Him. Sometimes we wonder if God caused something, or God allowed it. Either way, He can make the best of it. And so can we.

Have a positive attitude on the road to new life.

Discover God's best . . . on Route 66.

Possibilities

The following quote is attributed to Francis of Assisi from the twelfth century. It sounds like it might have originated in a modern seminar on leadership. Francis said, "Start doing what's necessary, then what's possible, and suddenly you're doing the impossible." People who have dreams might accomplish more of them if they followed that advice.

I have always been encouraged by Jesus' words about what is possible in life. With man, Jesus said, some things are impossible, but with God all things are possible (Matthew 19:26). Instead of putting limits on our dreams, we should put our dreams in God's hands—the God of possibilities.

Try the impossible on the road to new life.

Discover God's promises . . . on Route 66.

Faith

The late Arthur Watson was an executive with IBM and later U.S. ambassador to France. He had a humorous take on being too cautious in life: "Show me a man with both feet on the ground," he said, "and I'll show you a man who can't put his pants on."

Mr. Watson was saying that sometimes it is necessary to stand on one foot instead of two—to take a bit of a risk in life. If the apostle Peter had remained standing on both feet, he never would have climbed out of his boat and walked on the water to reach Jesus.

Be willing to step out in faith on the road to new life.

Discover God's divine provision . . . on Route 66.

Richness

Thomas Merton, who gave up a vocation in literary criticism to pursue God as a Trappist monk, wrote these challenging words: "The biggest human temptation is . . . to settle for too little." That thought reminds me of Paul's words in Ephesians where he says that God is able to do far more than anything we ask or think.

That is not a license to be irresponsible, of course, in testing God. But it is a challenge, as Thomas Merton wrote, to seek God's very best; not to settle for just getting by in life, but to experience God's richness in all our endeavors and circumstances.

Seek God's assistance on the road to new life.

Discover God's vast resources . . . on Route 66.

Full Trot

There is an Italian proverb that is a great spiritual metaphor. It says, "He who knows the road can ride at a full trot." When a horse and rider are on a road they've been down a hundred times, they can go at full speed. They can ride with confidence.

But in life, we are confronted with roads we've never been down before. And that can be intimidating. But guess who sees every bump and pothole in every road? God does. That's what it means to walk by faith and not by sight—to have confidence in God and not in ourselves.

Move ahead with confidence on the road to new life.

Discover God's knowledge of the road ahead . . . on Route 66.

Courage

Peter Drucker was one of the most famous management consultants of the twentieth century. He counseled major corporations in person and smaller ones through his many books. More interested in people than in factories, Drucker noted that "wherever you see a successful business, someone once made a courageous decision."

There is one courageous decision at the base of all others: the decision not to fail. In every area of life we must choose victory—and if we fail, we must choose to pick ourselves up and "press toward the goal for the prize of the upward call of God in Christ Jesus," to quote the apostle Paul (Philippians 3:14).

Be courageous on the road to new life.

Discover God's victory . . . on Route 66.

Safe Harbor

Sailors used to be unwilling to risk their lives on the open sea in a violent storm. So they would look for any harbor that offered shelter. And thus evolved the saying, "Any port in a storm," meaning any port is better than being in a dangerous storm.

People use the phrase today—"Any port in a storm"—to justify whatever will get them out of the trouble they're in. But that kind of situational ethic has no biblical base. It is far better to trust God to see you *through* the storm than to escape it in a port that is more dangerous than the storm itself.

Stay on the charted course on the road to new life.

Discover God's safe harbor . . . on Route 66.

Providence

You've heard this saying, I'm sure: "If you want it to rain, just plan a picnic." That's not exactly the same as Murphy's Law, but it is close. Life has a way of handing us the wrong thing at the wrong time. No wonder the motto of the Boy Scouts is "Be prepared."

James, one of the early apostles, had a wise perspective on planning for the future. He wrote that we should always preface our plans with this statement: "If it's the Lord's will" (James 4:15). That's not fatalism; it's faith! It's saying, "Nothing that happens will shake my confidence in God. I trust Him no matter what."

Desire God's will on the road to new life.

Discover God's providential protection . . . on Route 66.

Look for Lessons

Think about the things you remember from years, even decades, ago—a song, an event, a circumstance, or something someone said. More than likely, that memory has an emotional attachment like joy, sorrow, fear, excitement, pain, or relief. It was the famous Greek philosopher, Plato, who said, "All learning has an emotional base."

The Old Testament psalmist understood that as well. He wrote, "It is good for me that I have been afflicted, that I may learn Your statutes" (Psalm 119:71). As much as we don't like it, pain helps us learn. The next time you are experiencing discomfort, look for the lesson God wants you to learn.

Analyze life's lessons on the road to new life.

Discover God's teachable moments . . .
on Route 66.

Fix or Forget

The American poet Robert Frost said, "The reason worry kills more people than work is that more people worry than work." Since I can't verify that claim statistically, I'll go with this one instead: "Worry is like a rocking chair: Both give you something to do, but neither gets you anywhere." That is so true.

The older I get, the less I worry. Most things I could worry about are out of my control anyway. Jesus was right: Worry adds nothing to my life, so why bother? As for the things I can control, I would rather work on fixing them instead of worrying about them.

Overcome your worry on the road to new life.

Discover God's freedom from worry . . . on Route 66.

Fearless

One of the most daring Christian missionaries in the nineteenth century was Britain's David Livingstone. He explored the heart of the African continent and blazed a trail that others would later follow. Hacking his way through unexplored territory, he is famous for having said, "I will go anywhere provided it is forward."

That reminds me of the apostle Paul who, in his own missionary travels, was stopped twice by God before a third direction resulted in an open door. The secret is to keep moving forward. It is much easier for God to direct our path while we're moving than when we're standing still because of fear.

Be fearless on the road to new life.

Discover God's open doors on our journey . . . on Route 66.

Perseverance

Someone has said that the chief objection to gardening is that, by the time your back gets used to the pain, your enthusiasm is gone. Actually, that applies to lots of areas of life. We start off with a burst of speed and enthusiasm and then gradually begin to wonder if it was worth it at all.

The Bible says what's needed at those moments is perseverance. Yes, perseverance is even needed in the Christian life—especially in the Christian life. God lets us grow weary in order for us to see how much we need to rely on Him for strength to carry on.

Persevere on the road to new life.

Discover God's strength to carry on . . . on Route 66.

Meditation

Our fast-paced lifestyles can cause us to lose touch with a powerful spiritual discipline—the discipline of meditation on God and His Word. English statesman Edmund Burke once said, "To read without reflecting is like eating without digesting."

Biblical meditation is nothing more than dwelling upon God and His words and works. Of course, we can think about God at any time. But reflection, or meditation, is different in that we set aside extended quiet time to dwell upon God in His presence. The psalmist David wrote about using the quiet of the evening hours as a time to meditate upon God.

Take time to reflect on the road to new life.

Discover how to meditate on God . . . on Route 66.

Morality

The English philosopher John Locke, whose writings influenced many of America's founding fathers, once said, "To give a man full knowledge of true morality, I would send him to no other book than the New Testament." That is a surprising evaluation from someone who embraced only part of the New Testament's message.

There is great morality to be found in the New Testament—especially in the life of Jesus Himself. But to stop there would be to miss the greater point. The New Testament is not a guide to morality but an explanation for why our imperfect morality proves our need for a Savior.

Look for the greater point on the road to new life.

Discover God's view on morality . . . on Route 66.

True Contentment

Listen to these wise words: "The contented man is never poor; the discontented man is never rich." And here is what someone else wrote on the same topic: "Who is rich? He who is content. And who is that? Nobody." The writer's conclusion is a dramatic overstatement for effect, and his point is well made. There are very few truly content people in this world.

But there was one in the Bible. The apostle Paul said he had learned to be content in whatever condition he found himself (Philippians 4:11). Contentment can be learned—and today would be a good day to begin.

Set out on the road to new life.

Discover true contentment in God . . . on Route 66.

Satisfaction

In 1 Timothy 6, the apostle Paul mentioned two basic needs that we all have: food and clothing. He was making a point about material things—that it is possible to be content with the barest of essentials. But we really have many more needs than just food and clothes: we need encouragement, guidance, finances, wisdom, health, motivation, courage, and so on.

God is delighted to meet those needs as we orient our lives around Him. Paul also wrote these words to the Philippians: "My God shall supply all your need"— and *all* means *all* (Philippians 4:19). So take God at His Word and commit your needs to Him.

Be content on the road to new life.

Discover God's delight in meeting your needs . . . on Route 66.

Fulfillment

How would you describe the state of happiness— the state of being truly content? I like a definition of happiness that says, "Happiness is a way-station between too little and too much." To me, that suggests a person is happiest when he is focused on very important goals in life and has just what he needs to accomplish them.

The apostle Paul had a similar perspective when he said he had learned the secret of being content whether he had a little or had a lot. In other words, his happiness wasn't dependent on what he possessed but on being in God's will.

Experience fulfillment on the road to new life.

Discover God's secret of happiness . . . on Route 66.

The Mundane

I have heard it said that the man who never does anything he doesn't like rarely likes anything he does. Did you catch that? Let's face it—life is filled with mundane, non-exciting tasks that aren't much fun. So we need to figure out how to like even the things we don't like doing.

I think the secret is gratitude. Instead of disliking yard work, we could be grateful for having a house with a yard to care for. The apostle Paul said we should learn to "give thanks in all things" (1 Thessalonians 5:18). When we do, we will find reasons to like almost all of it.

Develop an attitude of gratitude on the road to new life.

Discover God's admonition to be thankful in all things . . . on Route 66.

Good News

Thomas Jefferson is quoted as saying he did not subscribe to a single newspaper nor even read one a month, and he found himself "infinitely the happier." Keeping up with the news is a fine line. We need to stay current on the affairs of the world, especially as they impact developing end-time events prophesied in the Bible. But following sensationalistic news shows or websites that thrive on bad news can have a negative impact on us.

Yes, there is bad news in the world, but there is much better news in Scripture—the good news of the Gospel of the kingdom of God.

Stay current on the road to new life.

Discover God's saving news . . . on Route 66.

Joy

Most of the time when we laugh, it's unplanned, the response to a surprise word or event. And laughter is good for the soul. But it's a mistake to confuse laughter with joy. The Christian writer Henri Nouwen has written, "We have to choose joy and keep choosing it every day. . . . Joy is the experience of knowing that you are unconditionally loved and that nothing—sickness, failure, emotional distress, oppression, war, or even death—can take that love away."

I encourage you today, and every day, to let your first choice be the choice of joy in the knowledge of God's love.

Be joyful on the road to new life.

Discover God's unconditional care for you . . . on Route 66.

God's Calling

You may be familiar with the words of Scottish Olympic sprinter Eric Liddell, who later became a Christian missionary in China. When explaining why he chose to be an athlete during his college years, he said, "I feel God's pleasure when I run."

Many people are afraid that God is going to call them to do something they won't enjoy if they surrender their lives to Him. But such is not the case. God created us and knows better than anyone what will bring us success and pleasure in life. There is no greater feeling than to feel God's pleasure in the work we do.

Delight in the road to new life.

Discover God's calling . . . on Route 66.

Silver Linings

I have heard it said that too many people miss the silver linings in life because they're always looking for gold. There is nothing wrong with expecting the best, of course, but gold is valuable mainly because it's rare. So if that's all we're looking for, we'll miss a lot of other valuables along the way.

When the Bible says to give thanks in everything, it means that in every situation in life there is something valuable to grasp—if we will look for it, embrace it, and be thankful. Even if it's nothing more than saying, "It could have been worse," that makes your present circumstance valuable!

Look for the silver linings on the road to new life.

Discover God's perspective . . . on Route 66.

Childlikeness

A Chinese philosopher who lived three centuries before the time of Christ made a wise observation about great men. He said, "The great man is he who has not lost the heart of a child." A few hundred years later, Jesus provided more clarity on the subject of childlikeness.

Jesus said that "whoever does not receive the kingdom of God as a little child will by no means enter it" (Mark 10:15). How do children receive gifts? With joy, with eagerness, with innocence, and without a shred of suspicion. Little kids are so grateful and exuberant and appreciative! Every Christian can receive God's gifts the same way—with open and honest hands.

Approach the road to new life with a childlike heart.

Discover God's gifts . . . on Route 66.

Laughter

A famous Swiss theologian, Karl Barth, was known not only for his profound writings but for his simple illustrations. He once said that "laughter is the closest thing to the grace of God." I don't know if it's the *closest* thing, but it is definitely close. Both laughter and grace are free, inviting, encouraging, powerful, and therapeutic.

The idea of laughter as therapy was first prescribed by Dr. Solomon nearly three thousand years ago. He said that a merry heart works like medicine. So if you want to feel better today, engage in some wholesome and graceful laughter. And spread it around!

Revitalize your heart on the road to new life.

Discover God's reasons to laugh . . . on Route 66.

Realizations

A couple was in a meeting with an architect to explore the possibility of building a new house. The more the architect talked about the cost of the new house, the better their old house looked. That kind of realization happens often, doesn't it? We suddenly realize just how fortunate we are in our present circumstances.

It's called contentment—and it's a hard perspective to develop in a culture that offers unlimited options. The apostle Paul offers the Bible's best words about contentment when he says he learned the secret of being content: "We brought nothing into the world, and we can take nothing out of it" (1 Timothy 6:7).

Realize what's important on the road to new life.

Discover God's reasons for contentment . . . on Route 66.

Rejoice

If you want to see a parent act like a child, just wait until a child achieves some success—in school, at a dance or piano recital, or carrying out a chore at home. There's clapping, high-fiving, and whoops of delight. Parents love to celebrate their children's successes.

Somehow, we adults forget to celebrate the same way with each other's successes. The apostle Paul wrote that we should rejoice with those who rejoice—and, by the way, weep with those who weep. A joy shared is a joy doubled, but a grief shared is a grief cut in half. Find someone to rejoice with today.

Celebrate on the road to new life.

Discover God's reasons to rejoice . . .
on Route 66.

A Whole Heart

When someone asked W. C. Fields why he was reading the Bible, he was said to have answered that he was looking for a loophole. Jesus Christ had little patience in His day for religious people who looked for ways to avoid obeying God. For example, some religious people avoided supporting their parents financially because they said their money had been dedicated to God—when it hadn't (Matthew 15:3-6).

A true sign of love for God is looking for reasons to meet His expectations, not avoid them. There is more joy to be found in serving God with a whole heart than with just half.

Look for ways to be obedient on the road to new life.

Discover the pleasure of serving God . . .
on Route 66.

No Worries

Did you hear about the man who was acting in an unusually good mood one day? A friend asked him why he was so happy, and the man replied, "I just realized this morning that I'm worried about so many things that if anything bad happens today, it will be two weeks before I'll be able to worry about it."

I'm all for not worrying, but for a different reason: Worry doesn't accomplish anything. Jesus reminded His disciples that worry would add nothing to their life; the same God who provides for creation will provide for them.

Get on the road to new life.

Discover God's reasons not to worry . . . on Route 66.

The Blues

I came across ten steps for getting rid of the blues on those days when things don't go right. Step number one is to do something nice for another person. Steps two through ten are to repeat step one nine more times for nine more people. What happens when we do things for others is that it changes our focus—we take our eyes off ourselves and our discouragement and put them on the needs of another person.

The Bible exhorts us to consider others' needs more important than our own. We help others and help ourselves at the same time.

Be generous on the road to new life.

Discover God's refocusing plan . . .
on Route 66.

Outlook

Konrad Adenauer was a German statesman who lived through the terrible years of World War II in Europe and was made the first Chancellor of the newly formed West Germany. His experiences with conflicting ideologies can be seen in this statement he made: "We all live under the same sky, but we don't all have the same horizon."

We're all human beings, but our attitudes and actions differ dramatically. What determines your outlook on life? Do you have an infallible guide that gives you perspective? The most reliable way to keep a positive attitude in life is to meditate on God's Word.

What is your viewpoint on the road to new life?

Discover God's purposes by meditating on His Word . . . on Route 66.

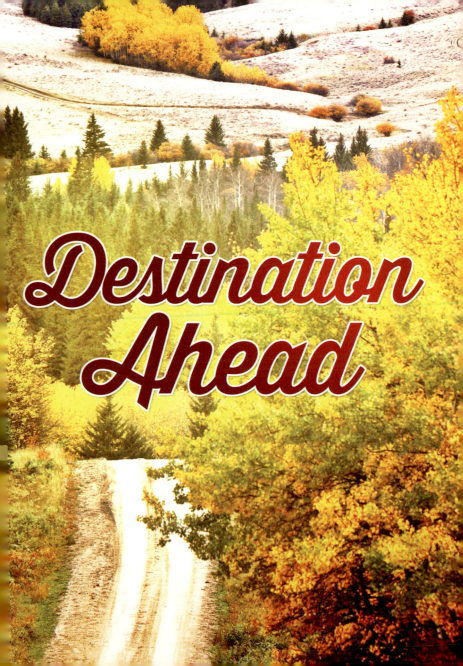

Destination Ahead

Freedom

One of the most misunderstood words in use today—especially among young people—is the word *freedom.* Too often, people think freedom means "the right to do whatever they want." But I agree with a Bible teacher who gave a better definition. Instead of freedom being "the right to do what I *want,*" freedom is "the power to do what I *ought.*"

Freedom is not the absence of restraints—God's rules are always in place and we are responsible for obeying them. Therefore, true freedom is when I have God's power to do what I should do, not what I want.

Do what is right on the road to new life.

Discover God's freedom . . . on Route 66.

Love Fully

The Italian astronomer Galileo wrote these important words: "I do not feel obliged to believe that the same God who has endowed us with sense, reason, and intellect, has intended us to forgo their use." In other words, our powers of reasoning are as important to God as our heart.

Jesus put it this way: We are to love God with all our heart, soul, mind, and strength (Mark 12:30). The totality of our being is to be used in loving and honoring God. If God has blessed you with a powerful mind, use it for His glory.

Glorify God on the road to new life.

Discover how to love God fully . . . on Route 66.

Something to Think On

In the early days of computers, the acronym G-I-G-O was often used. G-I-G-O stood for "garbage in, garbage out." If you wanted the computer to give accurate information, you had to give it accurate data. Good data in, good data out. Bad data in, bad data out.

The human mind is like a computer in that it mirrors the information we feed it. A verse in Proverbs captures this idea when it says, "As he thinks in his heart, so *is* he" (23:7). We become like what we think about. That's why the Bible says to think on those things that are true, noble, right, pure, lovely, and admirable.

Refine your thinking on the road to new life.

Discover God's frame of mind . . . on Route 66.

Creativity

The New York author Fran Lebowitz offers this advice to people who think they have artistic talent: "If you have a burning, restless urge to write or paint, simply eat something sweet and the feeling will pass." With all due respect, I have to disagree with Ms. Lebowitz.

You and I are made in the image of God. That means God's creativity is revealed in part through us, the pinnacle of His creation. Whether our creativity is appreciated by the world is not the point. The point is to express ourselves creatively in ways that glorify God, knowing that He will be well pleased.

Be inspired on the road to new life.

Discover God's creative image in you . . . on Route 66.

Rewarding Works

Blaise Pascal was a seventeenth-century Frenchman who was a mathematician, inventor, physicist, writer, philosopher, and theologian—a child prodigy who invented a mechanical calculator while just a teenager. Pascal knew something about reaping rewards for work done well. Yet it was Pascal who wrote, "Noble deeds that are concealed are most esteemed."

His biblical studies no doubt were the source of that truth since it was Jesus who cautioned against doing good works publicly to gain a reward. Jesus suggested that we can do our works publicly and receive the reward of men, or do them privately and receive God's reward (Matthew 6:1-4). I'm thinking God's rewards are always best.

Practice quiet good works on the road to new life.

Discover God's rewards . . . on Route 66.

Submission

At the end of the Civil War, General Robert E. Lee, commander of the Confederate Armies, said, "We have fought this fight as long, and as well as we know how. We have been defeated. For us, as a Christian people, there is now but one course to pursue. We must accept the situation."

That's an example of victory in defeat. Lee wasn't angry. He didn't rail against the victor. He didn't make excuses. He graciously accepted that his will wasn't going to prevail. Jesus did the same thing in the Garden of Gethsemane when He said, "Not My will, but Yours, be done."

Abandon your will on the road to new life.

Discover how to submit to God's will . . . on Route 66.

Ears to Hear

Language specialists estimate that there are nearly seven thousand distinct languages spoken in the world today. But there is one language that never appears on any official list of languages. And that is the language of the kingdom of heaven. In fact, sometimes people hear this language without really knowing it's a foreign language at all.

While speaking, Jesus would often say, "He who has ears to hear, let him hear!" He meant there is a difference between hearing God's words physically and hearing them spiritually. And to hear God's truth spiritually, we have to have what Jesus called "ears to hear."

Listen carefully on the road to new life.

Discover the language of God's kingdom . . . on Route 66.

First-Rate

Bertie Charles Forbes, better known as B. C. Forbes, was the Scottish-born founder of the American Forbes publishing empire and knew a little something about what constitutes good work. He once said, "There's more credit and satisfaction in being a first-rate truck driver than a tenth-rate executive."

I believe the apostle Paul also knew a little something about doing good work. He wrote in Colossians 3:23, "Whatever you do, do it heartily, as to the Lord." The job we have in life is not nearly as important as how we do the job—whether we are doing our best and doing it for the Lord.

Be a first-rate Christ-follower on the road to new life.

Discover how to work for God . . . on Route 66.

Habits

Someone has said that the dangerous thing about bad habits is that they start out like silken cobwebs and end up being like steel cables. Saint Augustine put it another way: "Habit, if not resisted, soon becomes necessity." But the good thing is that a bad habit can be replaced by a good habit.

A habit isn't necessarily good or bad. It is simply a repetitive thought or activity to which we have become accustomed or even dependent upon. In that case, good habits like Bible study, prayer, positive speech, kindness, exercise, healthy eating, and more are well worth cultivating.

Overcome bad habits on the road to new life.

Discover habits that will draw you close to God . . . on Route 66.

Extended Hands

The largest task ever assigned to a group of people in human history is the Great Commission—the task of making disciples of Jesus in all the nations. But He only gave His original disciples two specific instructions: baptize the new converts and teach them what I taught you. Everything else—how, when, and where—Jesus left up to them.

I find that amazing—that Jesus entrusted such a huge task to us with so few instructions. He obviously trusted His disciples, and us, to carry out the huge job of spreading the Gospel. Trust instills responsibility in those who are entrusted.

Begin your journey with God on the road to new life.

Discover the Great Commission . . . on Route 66.

Reaping and Sowing

We've all heard the saying, "The exception proves the rule." When something surprising happens—like when we get a warning instead of a ticket for exceeding the speed limit—it's an exception. We usually get the ticket and pay the fine! Even God allowed exceptions occasionally, like when He spared King David's life after his involvement in adultery and murder.

But here is God's rule: "Do not be deceived, God is not mocked; for whatever a man sows, that he will also reap" (Galatians 6:7). God never invites us to consider ourselves exceptions to His rules. We should live our lives taking God's words seriously.

Abide by God's principles on the road to new life.

Discover God's law of the harvest . . . on Route 66.

Stewardship

Novelist John A. Shedd made an observation about sailing ships that applies also to people. "A ship in harbor is safe," he wrote, "but that is not what ships are built for." How foolish it would be to spend money and creativity designing a beautiful ship, only to leave it anchored safely in the harbor.

Just as ships are for sailing, so men and women are for stewardship—being managers and servants of our Creator-God. Any human being not in a relationship with God and serving Him to accomplish His will is like a beautiful ship that never sails the seas.

Set sail on the road to new life.

Discover true fulfillment as a steward of God . . . on Route 66.

Seasoned Words

When you were growing up, at some point or another, you probably heard this admonition: "If you can't say something nice about a person, don't say anything at all." That's good advice, and it parallels another saying that comes to mind: "Gossip always seems to travel fastest over grapevines that are slightly sour."

Here's the Bible's take on the same theme: "Let your speech always *be* with grace, seasoned with salt" (Colossians 4:6). Salt adds flavor and keeps things from spoiling—not a bad goal for how we talk about others. Why not purpose today to make all your words be seasoned with the salt of grace.

Speak with grace on the road to new life.

Discover God's seasoned speech . . . on Route 66.

Purity

William Shakespeare had a character say something interesting in one of his plays. When given the chance to ask anything at all of the king, the character asked that he might never know any of the king's secrets. There are some things we're better off not knowing.

None of us is perfect, and we have all had our embarrassing or shameful moments. But increasingly, our goal should be to live a life that is "above reproach," to use the apostle Paul's description of spiritual elders. We should live the kind of life that does not fear being exposed, the kind of life that has nothing to hide.

Be blameless on the road to new life.

Discover God's purity . . . on Route 66.

Blueprint for Life

A writer named Josh Jenkins made this worthwhile observation about mistakes and failure: "To err is human," he said, "but when the eraser wears out ahead of the pencil, you're overdoing it." Sometimes in life, it feels like we've worn out the eraser long before the pencil is used up.

When that happens, it might be time to ask whether we are following God's plans and employing His wisdom. God doesn't want us to fail continually and consistently. He wants us to accomplish what He has gifted us to do. In order to write more than you erase, consult God's plans for abundant living in His Word.

Study your Bible on the road to new life.

Discover God's blueprint for life . . .
on Route 66.

Choices

Listen to the words of this ancient proverb: "He who wishes a fire must put up with the smoke." To me, this means that the best things in life aren't free— they require an investment of patience and often sacrifice.

There is a verse in the Bible that says something similar: If you want a clean barn, don't get an ox. But if you want a good harvest, an ox can make it happen (Proverbs 14:4). Life is filled with choices, and usually we have to give up something to get something else. It is a wise man or woman who is willing to sacrifice to achieve the very best in life.

Decisions must be made on the road to new life.

Discover God's choices . . . on Route 66.

Good Works

A medieval priest, Thomas à Kempis, once wrote the following: "At the Day of Judgment we shall not be asked what we have read but what we have done." He was not against reading, but was saying God is more concerned about how we live than what we know.

I believe, however, that when it comes to examining how we have lived, it will be obvious whether we have read one particular book, or not—that book being the Bible. For it is only in that book that we learn what it is God expects us to do for Him as followers of Christ.

Live by the Book on the road to new life.

Discover God's expectations . . . on Route 66.

Best Practices

American author Mark Twain had wise things to say on many topics, like this statement: "Do something every day that you don't want to do; this is the golden rule for acquiring the habit of doing your duty without pain." That is well said. The more we do a good thing that we often procrastinate about, the more quickly we see the benefits and how desirable it is to do it regularly.

Spiritual disciplines are that way—prayer, Bible study, worship, meeting together for fellowship. What at first seems like a chore soon becomes a joy—and we wonder why we ever put it off.

Develop discipline on the road to new life.

Discover God's best practices . . . on Route 66.

Diplomacy

I learned early in life how to be diplomatic around women: Never ask a woman her age and never forget her birthday. I was, therefore, pleased to read the words of the famous American poet, Robert Frost, who said, "A diplomat is a man who always remembers a woman's birthday but never remembers her age."

A spiritual diplomat is someone who is always sensitive to his surroundings; who is winsome and wise; who makes others feel accepted, comfortable, and appreciated. As ambassadors of Jesus Christ, Christians are called to be spiritual diplomats. Purpose to represent Him well today.

Be aware of your environment on the road to new life.

*Discover how to represent God . . .
on Route 66.*

Way of Life

Andrew Carnegie was the American industrialist who made a fortune in the steel industry and then made himself famous by giving most of it away to build libraries and other public facilities around the country. He once said, "As I grow older, I pay less attention to what men say. I just watch what they do."

The apostle James had a similar outlook. He said a Christian's good works are a reliable indicator of the genuineness of his faith (James 2:14-26). It's one thing to say we believe in Jesus, but it's another thing to *live* like Jesus. Try expressing your faith today without saying a word.

Exemplify godly conduct on the road to new life.

Discover God's leading . . . on Route 66.

Potential

Famous motivational speaker Zig Ziglar once said, "It's not what you've got, it's what you use that makes a difference." That's right in line with what scientists tell us about the human brain—we only use a small percentage of the brain's actual power. Just think how different the world would be if every person lived and worked to his or her full potential!

The Bible says we are "fearfully and wonderfully" made—a "marvelous work" of God's creative hand. Take a moment today to ask God to give you a fresh picture of your true potential.

Pursue excellence on the road to new life.

Discover your full potential in Christ . . . on Route 66.

Live Successfully

Three men were discussing the meaning of success.
One said, "Success would be serving as a consultant
to the president in the White House." The second
said, "No, success is being in a conversation with the
president when the red phone rings, but he chooses
not to answer it because he's talking to you." And
the third man said, "No, success is being in the Oval
Office when the red phone rings, having the president
answer it, and say, 'It's for you.'"

I would say the best definition of success is the one
Jesus used: accomplishing the work God gave Him to
do (John 17:4).

Employ yourself in the Lord's work on the road to
new life.

*Discover God's definition of success . . .
on Route 66.*

Anticipation

I found the following observation both compelling and convicting: "A servant is known by his master's absence." Think about parents who leave their teenage son at home alone while they are away for the weekend. They do that because they trust their son; they have confidence that their son will behave the same when they are away as he would if they were home.

Jesus Christ is our Master, and He is away right now—which says something about how He trusts us. The question is, What will He say when He returns?

Anticipate His return on the road to new life.

Discover God's prophetic promises . . .
on Route 66.

Faith Works

I can't count the number of times I have heard people say they hope their good deeds outweigh their bad deeds when it comes to going to heaven. The Bible says we can't get to heaven just by doing good deeds, but that we probably won't get there without them either.

Sound confusing? It isn't, really. Our good works are not the source of our salvation, but they are the fruit of it. Everyone who is truly saved by faith will be motivated to live a life that is pleasing to God—obeying His commands and serving Him through good works.

Let your faith produce works on the road to new life.

Discover God's transforming love . . . on Route 66.

Light in the Darkness

If you've ever been on a tour inside a cave, at some point the tour guide will switch off all the lights in order to demonstrate what true darkness is like. Deep below the earth, with no lights on, you literally can't see your hand in front of your face.

The only thing I know that is more unnerving than physical darkness is the complete absence of spiritual light. The Bible says the world is a dark place until the light of Christ is introduced. And those who know Jesus are to be His light in the world.

Be a light on the road to new life.

Discover God's power over darkness . . . on Route 66.

Witness

In courtroom trials you'll hear the attorneys say: "Objection! Calls for speculation by the witness!" And the judge usually sustains the objection. Why? Because a witness is allowed to say only what he knows. In other words, only what he has seen and heard.

The apostle John wrote to early Christians about what he had "seen and heard" concerning Christ. In other words, he was an eyewitness, and therefore reliable. You and I haven't seen Jesus personally, but we can still be witnesses for Him by declaring what we know and how we *have* seen Him change our life.

Testify to what you have seen and heard on the road to new life.

Discover how to witness for Christ . . . on Route 66.

Credibility

A major dental research organization once published a study that showed that chocolate is actually beneficial in fighting plaque and cavities in teeth. You probably need to know, however, that 90 percent of the money for the study came from one of America's largest chocolate candy companies.

The word "credibility" comes to mind, doesn't it? It should also come to mind concerning our Christian testimony. Is what we say about being a Christian supported by our actions? That is, does our walk match our talk? We can either help or hinder the cause of Christ based on how we live.

Be a walking testimony on the road to new life.

Discover God's sustaining support in your life . . . on Route 66.

Living Letters

The twenty-one letters in the New Testament are called epistles, a name that comes from a Greek word that means "to send a message." While more people use email than write letters today, there's one kind of epistle that will never be replaced: the living epistle.

Christians are living epistles from God to the rest of the world. The message we are carrying to everyone is the good news that God loves them and has sent Jesus Christ into the world to forgive their sins. If you are a Christian, make sure your letter is open and easy to read.

Make your message accessible on the road to new life.

Discover the letter God is writing through you . . . on Route 66.

Evidence

Sir William Blackstone was an eighteenth-century English professor who is famous for his commentaries on English law and for "Blackstone's Formulation"—the idea that it is better for ten guilty people to go free than for one innocent person to suffer.

Blackstone's Formulation is all about evidence. And it raises an interesting question for Christians: If you or I were accused of being a Christian in a court of law, would there be enough evidence to convict us? If someone looked at our checkbook, our calendar, our Bible, our knees, would they say, "Guilty as charged!" or "Insufficient evidence"?

Review your evidence on the road to new life.

Discover God's verdict . . . on Route 66.

Giving Conditions

Most of us have been approached by someone on the street who asks for money; but from the person's appearance, we are not sure our gift will be used in the best way.

In those situations, I'm reminded of how my "appearance" must have looked to God when He decided to offer me the gifts of forgiveness and salvation. Unconditional giving is not based on anticipated outcomes; it is based on a heart of compassion that seeks to meet a need. We can't always be sure how our gifts will be used, but we can be sure of one thing: our willingness to give.

Be compassionate on the road to new life.

Discover God's unconditional gifts . . . on Route 66.

Clothed in Love

Depending on where you are in the world, you might recognize leaders of various religions: Jewish elders in the Old City of Jerusalem, a Hindu holy man chanting on the banks of the Ganges, a Muslim mullah leading prayers in a mosque in Iraq, or Buddhist monks in their saffron-colored robes in Tibet.

But what about Christians? How are they supposed to be identified? Jesus Christ said, "By this all will know that you are My disciples, if you have love for one another" (John 13:35). When Christians leave home each day, they are to be clothed in love for all the world to see.

Be identified on the road to new life.

Discover God's adornment in your life . . . on Route 66.

Impact

Benjamin Franklin remains a household name more than two hundred years after his death. To be remembered after your death, Franklin said you must either write things worth reading or do things worth writing about—and he seems to have done both.

Being remembered is a worthy goal, but not for reasons of fame. Instead, the legacy we leave behind for our children and others is definitely worth considering. It's not important that people write books about us. But it is important that they be encouraged to live a good and godly life because of being touched by the life we lived.

Make a positive impact on the road to new life.

Discover God's ways to impact lives for eternity . . . on Route 66.

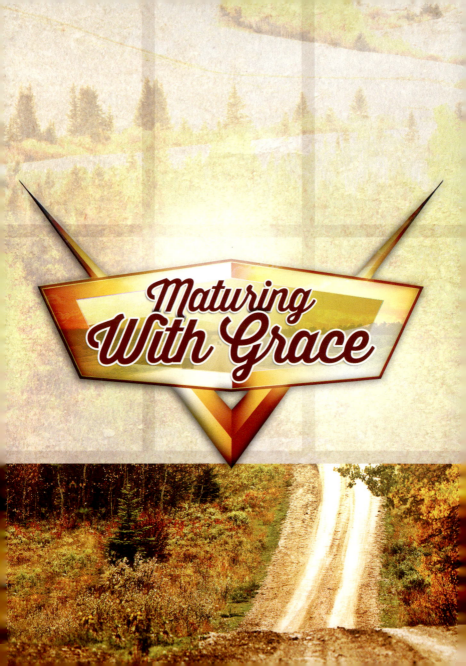

Effort

When was the last time you stood by a beautiful waterfall and watched the stream and the falls flowing uphill instead of downhill? The answer is "Never." Everything in life flows downhill naturally, including the quality of our lives if we're not careful. It takes effort to pump water uphill, and it takes effort to climb higher on the ladder of spiritual maturity as well.

The apostle Paul used words like "diligence," "work," "train," and "discipline" to describe the effort it takes on our part to grow in grace. That's not a contradiction. God provides the grace, and we provide the response in terms of diligence.

Travel uphill on the road to new life.

Discover God's sustaining power . . . on Route 66.

Spiritual Babes

The great English man of letters, Samuel Johnson, wrote that "babies do not want to hear about babies; they like to be told of giants and castles."

The apostle Paul addressed a group of spiritual babes in the church at Corinth. But he didn't pump them up by calling them wonderful and amazing. He told them exactly what they were: spiritual infants who weren't growing in Christ. In the spiritual life, as in real life, we have to crawl, then walk, then run. But if we are still crawling when we should be running, we have to be honest and implement a plan for growth.

Sprint toward God on the road to new life.

Discover God's path to maturity . . . on Route 66.

Challenge

Edmund Burke was one of England's most famous statesmen. His adult life was spent in the realm of political philosophy. So I wasn't surprised when I read these words of his: "He who wrestles with us strengthens our nerves and sharpens our skill. Our antagonist is our helper."

That is a perfect, practical illustration of the truth expressed in Proverbs 27:17: "As iron sharpens iron, so a man sharpens the countenance of his friend." We need people around us who will challenge us, disagree with us, and correct us. It's one of the ways God uses to help us grow up before we grow old.

Appreciate challenges on the road to new life.

Discover God's tools for growth . . . on Route 66.

Work in Progress

Construction on the Eiffel Tower in Paris began in 1887 and was completed two years later. I have seen an art poster that shows six photographs taken from the same vantage point during the construction. The first photo shows the foundation, the last photo shows the completed tower, and the four photos in between show it getting gradually taller—one piece of iron at a time.

The poster reminds me that growth takes time—but growth will happen if we persevere faithfully, one step and choice at a time. God promises that He will complete the good work He began in us through Christ Jesus.

Be a "work in progress" on the road to new life.

Discover God's complete work in you . . . on Route 66.

Maturity

One of the most well-known verses in the New Testament is 1 Corinthians 13:11: "When I was a child, I spoke as a child, I understood as a child, I thought as a child; but when I became a man, I put away childish things." Paul is referring to spiritual maturity in this verse, but there is a principle involved that goes further.

Children have many lovable traits, but they're also impulsive, have temper tantrums, don't like hard jobs, live only for the moment, and think the world revolves around them. Hopefully, as adults, we have learned to put away those kinds of childish things.

Become a spiritual adult on the road to new life.

Discover God's plan for maturity in Him . . . on Route 66.

Fear

Neal Armstrong, the American astronaut and first person to walk on the moon, said, "Fear is not an unknown emotion to us"—referring to himself and his fellow astronauts. Fear was something to be managed calmly like all the other variables in a trip to the moon.

Maturity doesn't mean never feeling fear. It means understanding fear and controlling it rather than it being in control. The Bible would not frequently say, "Fear not," if keeping fear at bay were not possible. Fear usually arises from a lack of knowledge. But because God knows the future, we don't have to live in fear.

Take control of your fear on the road to new life.

Discover God's infinite knowledge . . . on Route 66.

Lifetime of Discovery

American historian and philosopher Will Durant, along with his wife, Ariel, wrote an exhaustive, eleven-volume history of civilization. In his sunset years, he made this observation: "Sixty years ago I knew everything; now I know nothing; education is a progressive discovery of our own ignorance."

That reminds me of the apostle Paul's experience. As a young Pharisee, he thought he knew everything; but when he met Christ, he realized he knew little of what was truly important. And he made knowing Christ his lifelong goal. God is an infinite subject, and those who truly know Him readily admit how much more they have to learn.

Journey on the road to new life.

Discover God for a lifetime . . . on Route 66.

Retirement

The late British scientist Alex Comfort once said that "two weeks is about the ideal length of time to retire." A two-week retirement would be about the same as a two-week vacation during which we transition from one vocation to another—from the vocation of our income-producing years to the vocation of our service-focused years.

For the Christian, there is no retirement from service to Christ. If we have the privilege of being able to support ourselves without working in our senior years, that simply means we have more time available for serving Christ and serving others in His name.

Never retire from service on the road to new life.

Discover God's plan for your senior years . . . on Route 66.

Spiritual Education

See if you agree with this observation:
Education is what you get when your parents
send you to college, but it isn't manifested in you
until you send your children. One of the sure
signs of education or enlightenment is our desire
to help others toward the same goal.

The apostle Paul understood this. In his second
letter to his young protégé, Timothy, he told
Timothy to take what he had been taught and
pass it on to faithful people who could then teach
others. Where are you in that chain of spiritual
education? Are you learning? Are you teaching
others?

Start a chain reaction on the road to new life.

*Discover God's plan for spiritual education
. . . on Route 66.*

Identity

The British writer Logan Pearsall Smith once wrote, "Don't laugh at a young person for his changing behaviors. He's only trying on one face after another till he finds his own." It is sometimes amusing to watch young people search for their identity, but it is not amusing to see adults doing the same thing.

To discover who we are, we have to ask the only one who knows: the God who created us. God knows every man, woman, and child intimately and wants to say, "First of all, you are My child. Now let Me help you discover who I created you to be."

Acquire a sense of personal identity on the road to new life.

Discover who God created you to be . . . on Route 66.

Application

Benjamin Franklin commented about a man who was so learned that he knew the word for "horse" in nine different languages, but so unlearned that he bought a cow to ride on. Mr. Franklin often used proverbial language to make his point, and here I think the point is the difference between education and true knowledge, or wisdom.

And that point applies to the Christian life as well. We can know the facts of the Bible from Genesis to Revelation, but if we aren't applying the Bible to our lives, we have missed the whole point—we gain knowledge but lack wisdom.

Pursue wisdom on the road to new life.

Discover how to apply God's Word in your life . . . on Route 66.

Knowledge

The Book of Proverbs is the most practical book ever written about education, mainly because it is more concerned with wisdom than knowledge. But also because of its priorities. For instance, there is a beautiful passage at the beginning of chapter 2 that talks about the rigorous pursuit of knowledge—how we must search diligently for knowledge like we would search for hidden treasure.

And then it describes the payoff—what we get for our efforts in pursuit of knowledge. Then, Proverbs 2:5 says that you will discover the knowledge of God. Only the knowledge of God gives value to all other branches of knowledge.

Diligently seek God on the road to new life.

Discover the knowledge of God . . . on Route 66.

Repetition

You and I have forgotten a lot that we used to know. Perhaps it is an algebraic formula from a math class, or a telephone number, or the words of a hymn. The saying is definitely true, "Out of sight, out of mind." We eventually forget those things we stop using.

The author of Psalm 119 said that he continually set God's judgments before him so he could walk in them. And he used the nighttime hours, watching the sheep, as a way to meditate on God's Word. In order to know and remember the truth of God's Word, we must continually keep it before us.

Persistently study the Bible on the road to new life.

Discover God's promises through the study of His Word . . . on Route 66.

Fear of God

James Barrie, the English author who gave us the childhood fantasy of Peter Pan, once said, "I am not young enough to know everything." I think he meant what we all come to realize as we get older—that we weren't quite as all-knowing as we thought we were when we were young.

The Bible speaks highly of the aging process and the wisdom it brings. But there is an even more important source of wisdom, the Book of Proverbs says, and that is the fear of God. As we respect and honor God for who He is, we gain a greater understanding of who we are.

Fear the Lord on the road to new life.

Discover the foundation for godly wisdom . . . on Route 66.

Old Age

I have heard it said that for the unlearned man, old age is like the winter; but for the wise man, old age is the harvest. Personally, I have never been more excited about the work God has given me to do. I have spent many years acquiring knowledge and hopefully a bit of wisdom. I finally feel like I'm becoming qualified to make a contribution!

No one should resist growing old. Use today to acquire as much knowledge and wisdom as you can, and then ask God to give you a place to put it to good use for all your years on earth.

Welcome the harvest season on the road to new life.

Discover God's workplace in your "season" of life . . . on Route 66.

Temptation

I once read a piece of humorous advice about temptation. It said, "Don't worry about avoiding temptation. As you grow older, it starts avoiding you." That contradicts what one of my seminary professors said—he was around seventy years old at the time—when one of his students asked him at what point in life temptations of the flesh cease to be a problem. "I don't know," the professor replied, "but it must be sometime after age seventy!"

I agree with the professor's sentiment: We're never too old to be tempted. As long as Satan is roaming about, we have to live an alert and protected life.

Shield yourself from the enemy on the road to new life.

Discover God's hedge of protection . . . on Route 66.

Aging

There was an article in a national magazine about seniors who are returning to the workforce. One boss commented on how it would take two or three younger workers to replace his best senior employee. But he was looking—after all, she was ninety-five years old.

Now that's what I call a breath of fresh air! For too long, our culture has been trying to invent the Fountain of Youth. Instead, we may be discovering a Fountain of Wisdom in those who have lived long and lived well. The Bible suggests that with many years comes much wisdom for living.

Embrace the road to new life.

Discover God's perspective on aging . . . on Route 66.

Elders

There is a reason the Bible refers to church leaders as "elders"—in that culture, they were elder! That is, they were older men who had demonstrated wisdom and godliness over a span of time so they could serve as examples for younger Christians. And Paul assigns the same trait of exemplary living to older women who serve as models for younger women.

Our goal in life should be not only to grow "older" but to grow "elder"—that is, to develop a reputation for maturity and wisdom, to be an example for younger people to follow. As you grow older today, grow elder as well.

Be a model Christ-follower on the road to new life.

Discover how God defines maturity . . . on Route 66.

Teaching

Anyone who has ever been a teacher knows that teaching others is the best way to become confident about what you believe. When you teach others, you teach yourself. When you convince others, you convince yourself. When you persuade others, you become persuaded yourself.

The most confident, mature Christians I know are those who are involved in building up others in the faith. They teach Sunday school or a Bible study or lead a small group or are involved in evangelism or discipling their own children. The best way to remain strong in your faith is to make others strong with what you believe.

Prepare others for the road to new life.

Discover God's blessings on teachers . . . on Route 66.

Fruit-full

In Southern California, we are blessed with fresh fruit year round. But even with advances in plant breeding, botanists have still not been able to create a tree that will grow several kinds of fruit at once. But there is a tree in God's spiritual garden that will.

Every Christian has the ability to produce at least nine kinds of fruit in his or her life—the Bible calls them the fruit of the Spirit. They are the characteristics that Jesus Christ demonstrated in His life while on earth. And they should be evident in all who believe in Him.

Exhibit godly characteristics on the road to new life.

Discover God's "fruit stand" in your life . . . on Route 66.

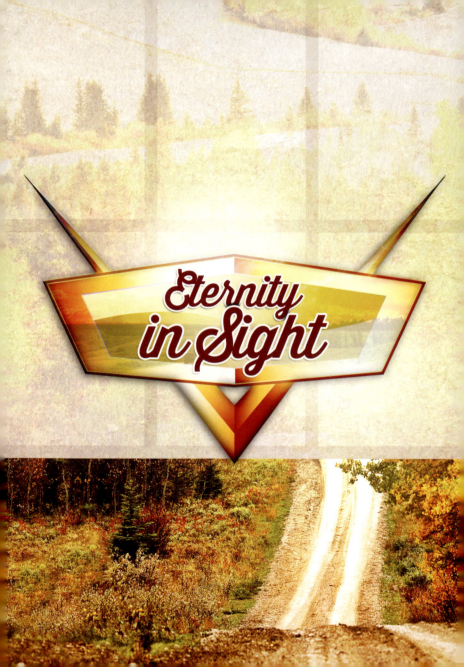

End of Time

Scientists are increasing their efforts to harness the strongest, most dependable, most unstoppable force of energy on earth: the surging ocean tides. Twice a day in most places, tides come in and go out like clockwork around the world. The regularity of the tides gave rise to the famous observation that "time and tide wait for no man."

We can no more stop the tides than we can stop time. And time moves on God's schedule, not ours. If you haven't thought about the march of time lately, do so today—mainly to be sure you are ready for time to end and eternity to begin.

Now is the time to get on the road to new life.

Discover God's timetable . . . on Route 66.

World Government

Among many descriptions of democracy are these two that I like: Democracy is where the people choose the person who will ultimately get the blame. And this one: Democracy is the worst form of government except for all the other forms that have already been tried.

But there is one form of government that hasn't been tried that will be better than all the rest: rule by the King of kings, the Lord Jesus Christ. The Bible says He is going to rule the world for a thousand years after His Second Coming (Revelation 20:6). And there will be no blame since His rule will be perfect.

Look ahead on the road to new life.

Discover God's future reign . . . on Route 66.

Book of Life

You have probably heard the saying that if something isn't in writing, it doesn't exist. A corollary is that I can forget and you can forget, but a piece of paper never forgets. Putting things in writing makes them as permanent as they can be.

God writes things down, too. Psalm 139 says that God wrote down all the days of our lives in His book before they came to pass. The Bible also says God has a book in which are written all the names of those who are going to heaven. And we can be assured that what is written in God's books is never forgotten.

The Christian's name will never be forgotten on the road to new life.

Discover God's library of eternal life . . . on Route 66.

Heavenly Home

If you've ever built or remodeled a house, you've learned the wisdom of these words: "When undertaking any major home building project, make a very generous budget—then double it!" In other words, we are not always realistic about what things cost.

The most realistic book I have ever read is the Bible. It does not cover up the damage caused by man's sinfulness or what it cost God to set things right. It cost God the life of His only Son, Jesus Christ. Included in that price is a heavenly home He is building for all those who trust in Christ (John 14:2).

Realism is often disturbing on the road to new life.

Discover the price God paid for our heavenly prospects . . . on Route 66.

Waiting

The American playwright Samuel Behrman said that there are two kinds of people in our lives. There are the people who keep us waiting and the people who have to wait on us. Everyone in life is waiting on *someone* or *something*. And Christians are waiting on both: They are waiting on the Second Coming of Christ and the establishment of His kingdom on earth.

The apostle Peter predicted there would be scoffers in the last days who say that Christians are waiting on nothing, that Jesus isn't going to return (2 Peter 3:3-4). But I'd rather be waiting on Him to return than have Him waiting on me to believe.

Wait expectantly on the road to new life.

Discover the promise of Christ's return . . . on Route 66.

Warning

I once read some good advice about childrearing that said: "Never threaten a child. Either punish him or forgive him." But, you ask, didn't God threaten the Israelites in the Old Testament? No, God warned them so they would be aware of the consequences of their choices.

Some people don't take God's warnings seriously. Would God really judge people who reject His offer of salvation? Jesus seemed to think so. His words, recorded in the Gospel of John, are that the judgment of God will rest on all who reject God's gift of forgiveness and eternal life. It's not a threat, but it *is* a warning.

Accept the gift of salvation on the road to new life.

Discover the reality of God's judgment . . . on Route 66.

Possessions

It has often been said that a person is rich according to what he *is,* not according to what he *has.* While the Bible does not condemn material wealth, it does suggest the value of being rich in other things as well. The apostle Paul exhorts us to be rich in good works, while James' letter talks about being rich in faith. Those are the kinds of wealth Jesus said to accumulate in heaven where no one can take them away.

Regardless of how much money you have, the most valuable form of wealth is that which comes from and is shared from the heart.

Accumulate eternal wealth on the road to new life.

Discover God's true riches . . . on Route 66.

Destination: Heaven

The late comedian Rodney Dangerfield once said he had discovered the only way to look thin without dieting: Hang out with people who weigh more than you do! That reminds me of people who think they can get into heaven because they have sinned less than others.

There are only two ways to get to heaven: Never sin a single time in your entire life, or know someone who never sinned and who will take the punishment for your sins and allow you to enter heaven as if you had lived perfectly yourself—which is exactly what Jesus Christ did for us (2 Corinthians 5:21).

Determine your destination on the road to new life.

Discover God's requirement for heavenly citizenship . . . on Route 66.

Important Meeting

Back when gas stations had attendants, a pastor joined a long line of cars waiting to be filled on a Friday afternoon. When it was the pastor's turn, the attendant apologized for the delay, saying people always waited until the last minute to prepare for trips. "I understand," the pastor said. "It's the same in my business."

We make preparations daily for life's important meetings and moments. But many people are failing to prepare for the most important meeting of all: standing before God. The Bible tells us how to get ready for that meeting—don't fail to prepare before it's too late.

Use your time wisely on the road to new life.

Discover how to prepare to meet God . . . on Route 66.

Inheritance

We've all heard it said that where there's a will, there's a way. But I've also heard it said that where there's a will, there are relatives. It's always been good for a laugh in movies and television—nervous relatives gather in an attorney's office for the reading of the will of a deceased, very rich relative, hoping they've been granted an inheritance.

Did you know that, if you are a Christian, you have been granted an inheritance far greater than any on earth? You have been made a member of God's family, a fellow-heir of Jesus Christ, set to inherit all the riches of the Father for all eternity.

If you haven't already done so, join God's family on the road to new life.

Discover God's eternal inheritance . . . *on Route 66.*

Spiritual Investments

Mark Twain once warned that if you're going to put all your eggs in one basket, you'd better keep an eye on the basket. Modern investment counselors have the same advice: Diversify; only invest a small portion of your assets in any one investment.

That may be good investing advice in an uncertain economy, but it's bad advice when investing in eternity. Jesus Christ said He was *the* way to eternal life and no one comes to God except through Him (John 14:6). The apostle Peter said there is no other name under heaven by which we can be saved (Acts 4:12). My advice? Invest your whole heart in Jesus.

Be single-minded on the road to new life.

Discover God's investment plan . . .
on Route 66.

Treasures

Here is an epitaph on a gravestone that makes biblical sense: "What I kept for myself, I no longer have. What I gave away to others, I have now and always will." We're often told, "You can't take it with you." But if we use what we have on earth to glorify God, there will be treasure waiting for us in heaven.

Jesus made that clear, of course, in His well-known words about laying up treasures in heaven instead of on earth. Things done on earth for the sake of heaven are the only things we will find rewarded when we get there.

Commit your works to heaven on the road to new life.

Discover God's future rewards . . . on Route 66.

Legacy

Jules Renard was a nineteenth-century French author who wrote in a very humanistic fashion. But I find one of his observations insightful. He wrote, "The reward of great men is that, long after they have died, one is not quite sure that they are dead." He is talking, of course, about one's legacy—that part of us that lives on past our death.

Legacies take many forms. Our children represent our legacy to the next generation, as can our work and our ministry for Christ. It is worth considering: What am I doing now that will continue to bear fruit into eternity?

Plant seeds on the road to new life.

Discover God's ways to leave a lasting legacy . . . on Route 66.

MOMENTS
WITH GOD ON

Route 66